Merton P. Strommen

THE INNO- VATIVE CHURCH

Seven Steps to Positive
Change in Your
Congregation

Augsburg
MINNEAPOLIS

Other books by Merton P. Strommen:

Author:

Bridging the Gap
Five Cries of Youth
Profiles of Church Youth

Coauthor:

Five Cries of Grief
Five Cries of Parents
Five Shaping Forces
How Church-Related Are Church-Related Colleges?
Ministry in America
A Study of Generations
Ten Faces of Ministry

Editor:

Research on Religious Development:
A Comprehensive Handbook

To Shelby Andress, my associate at Search Institute,
who helped develop and put into practice many of the
concepts described in this book

THE INNOVATIVE CHURCH
Seven Steps to Positive Change in Your Congregation

Cover design by David Meyer
Text design by James Satter

Library of Congress Cataloging-in-Publication Data

Strommen, Merton P.
   The innovative church : seven steps to positive change in your congregation / Merton P. Strommen.
     p.   cm.
     Includes bibliographical references.
     ISBN 0-8066-3573-8 (alk. paper)
     1. Pastoral theology. 2. Organizational change. 3. Change—Religious aspects—Christianity. I. Title.
BV4011.S92   1997
253—dc21   97-18429
                                                              CIP

Manufactured in the U.S.A.   AF 9-3573

01 00 99 98 97   1 2 3 4 5 6 7 8 9 10

CONTENTS

94135

PREFACE

THIS BOOK ADDRESSES AN ISSUE that is challenging for most pastors and lay leaders: How do I best introduce the changes required by my congregation to meet today's emerging needs?

We assume the changes do not involve the changeless message of Jesus Christ. Nor do they involve altering God's mission, made incarnate by Jesus Christ and entrusted to his church. The changes involve the way this message is shared in today's society.

The purpose of this book is to show how a congregation best goes about making significant changes in its ministry. It presents a process that develops a congregation's readiness to act as needs arise.

The need for making changes is not unique to religious organizations. The need appears in every area of society—schools, health care, government, business, law enforcement, and welfare. For that reason much of what is shared in this book can be applied to any organization. But my primary focus is on the congregation, with special reference to its unique quality—that it is both a human and a divine organization.

Throughout the book, reference is made to this unique characteristic of a congregation. Its human and divine qualities interact to influence each other. Although acknowledging the importance of being God-centered and relying on God's guidance and power, the book focuses primarily on the human factors in congregational life—factors that can facilitate or hinder the work of a congregation.

An important characteristic of this book is its use of research from the Innovation Study, which looked at adults serving in five national youth organizations.[1] The research, done over a five-year period, is unique in that it was designed to identify the underlying factors in people's attempt to effect needed change. Through the use of complex analyses of data gained from broad national samples, we were able to isolate twenty factors that facilitate or hinder the making of needed change. The twenty factors fall into five major areas (see sidebar P.1).

```
┌─────────────────────────────────────────────────────┐
│                    SIDEBAR P.1                        │
│          Factors that Facilitate or Hinder Change     │
├─────────────────────────────────────────────────────┤
│                                                       │
│    1. ATMOSPHERE (conduciveness to change)            │
│       Commitment to change                            │
│       Support for innovation                          │
│       Encouragement of creativity                     │
│       Team spirit                                     │
│       Organizational pride                            │
│                                                       │
│    2. GROUP SKILLS (for effecting change)             │
│       Listening to needs                              │
│       Planning with needs as focus                    │
│       Preparing carefully for change                  │
│       Communicating with constituencies               │
│       Training to enhance competencies                │
│                                                       │
│    3. VALUES (that promote needed change)             │
│       Insisting on quality                            │
│       Pressing for results                            │
│       Focusing on mission                             │
│       Expanding participation                         │
│       Creating a positive image                       │
│                                                       │
│    4. RESISTANCES TO CHANGE                           │
│       Skepticism over anything new                    │
│       Protectiveness of current situation             │
│       Contentment with status quo                     │
│       Tension within                                  │
│                                                       │
│    5. MOTIVATION TO CHANGE                            │
│                                                       │
└─────────────────────────────────────────────────────┘
```

These factors do not change, as do people's opinion of their current president. Rather, they have remained the same since they were first reported in a technical publication, *Five Shaping Forces*. That is why I have used them to undergird the conceptual model introduced in this book and to provide information on innovation and change available from measures of the twenty factors. A cross-validation study carried out three years after the first survey established the validity of findings reported in this book.

(For further information on the scope and scientific integrity of the study, Appendix A.)

In addition to the findings from this five-year Innovation Study, I draw from other research that provides corroboration and added insight. I draw also on the writings of consultants whose expertise in the field of planned change adds much to our understanding of how to introduce change.

I intend to go beyond sharing information on innovation and the best way to effect significant change. My ultimate purpose is to help congregations address innovation as a natural part of their organizational life and to achieve the ideal: members who are predisposed to respond creatively to the needs that surround them.

OVERVIEW OF THE BOOK

This book shows how a pastor or lay leader can foster positive congregational response to emerging needs. The approach is based on a conceptual plan documented in the Innovation Study. It provides convincing evidence of advances that can occur in congregations when the plan is put into practice.

The first part of this book presents an analysis of the innovation process by showing the need for innovative churches and why congregations resist change. It identifies why it is difficult to effect needed change. The difficulty centers in obstacles common to all organizations. These obstacles influence the way individuals, organizations, people in various geographic areas, and cultural groups respond to change.

When it comes to congregations, however, the obstacles to innovation include more than human factors common to all organizations. The obstacles include also the opposition of sinister and real spiritual forces.

An essential ingredient for making significant changes within a congregation is a task force of committed people who function as a learning or ministry team. This team of seven or eight people can limit its focus to one vision, one innovation, and stay with its task until the team has brought about a lasting change. These people are best able to introduce innovations and make real their congregation's visions.

The second part of this book focuses on the seven steps for positive change in a congregation. The seven steps are:

F   Free people to participate in effecting change
U   Unite around needs
T   Tie innovation to mission and values
U   Use input of legitimizers
R   Rally broad ownership
E   Engage in action
S   Sustain the innovation long-term

These steps are effective not only in bringing about needed change but also in developing over time a readiness to respond to needed change. This readiness is stimulated by a style of leadership that frees in people a willingness and desire to participate. It creates a culture where innovation is welcomed and members are supported in their efforts to be creative.

The motivation to innovate originates in an awareness of need that in turn creates a feeling of obligation to act. When this awareness is coupled with a clear and compelling sense of congregational mission, one can expect to see progressive and lasting changes in the approach of members to needed ministries. We found this to be true in the Innovation Study. We also found that the most powerful predictor of innovative congregations is a strong sense of mission.

A key step is gaining the support of legitimizers (people whose approval and support are needed if change is to be made) and involving whatever constituency groups may be impacted by a proposed innovation. The purpose is to gain people's counsel and psychological ownership in what is being introduced. Another purpose is to teach by modeling how a congregation can address need and launch new ministries.

To be effective, a task force needs to learn how to work together as a ministry team, to seek God's guidance, and, in general, to grow in its ability to carry out the ministry of Jesus Christ. If the innovation is to be sustained, its work must be long range and visionary.

ACKNOWLEDGMENTS

I am especially grateful to Shelby Andress, director of consulting services at Search Institute, who helped carry out the research project that undergirds this book. She was to have been coauthor of this book, but due to the extended illness and subsequent death of her husband, she was not able to take on this additional responsibility.

I am indebted to the following people whose reviews of various versions of this manuscript helped me immensely. They include seminary professors Roland Martinson and Paul Berge; Search Institute president Peter Benson; church executives Richard Gahl and Paul Krentz; Bishop Peter Strommen; lawyer James Strommen; Dick Hardel, director of Augsburg Youth and Family Institute; Christian education director David Zellar; and parish pastors Rebecca Ellenson, Thomas Zarth, Timothy Strommen, and Luther Strommen.

Thanks also to Pat Samples, under whose guidance we at Search Institute arrived at the acronym FUTURES for visualizing the steps in our conceptual model.

And special thanks to the editorial staff of Augsburg Fortress, Ronald Klug and Beth Ann Gaede, for their wise counsel and expertise. They enhanced the readability of this book.

My deep appreciation to:

• Twenty wonderful youth leaders (acknowledged in Five Shaping Forces) whose five cooperating institutions made the Innovation Study possible.

• Dr. Milo Brekke, whose technical skill as Principal Research Scientist at Search Institute guided the complex computer analyses.

• Lutheran Brotherhood for its generous computer grant and the National Institute of Mental Health for funding the Innovation Study.

PART ONE

UNDERSTANDING INNOVATION

CHAPTER ONE

THE NEED FOR INNOVATIVE CHURCHES

"He who was seated on the throne said, 'I am making everything new!'"

—*Revelation 21:5*

AS A CONGREGATIONAL LEADER, you face a host of new issues, many of which did not shout for attention a few decades ago. Now these issues sit on the doorstep of your congregation, clamoring for attention.

Some time ago I noticed an article in one of my professional journals about a workshop held in California. The workshop was unique in that it included Russian psychologists who serve as family therapists in the former Soviet Union. When they were asked to name the most pressing family problems they face, they drew up this list: infidelity and jealousy, conflicts over everyday responsibilities, conflicting values on child rearing, alcoholism, intergenerational conflict, sex, single parenting, divorce, teenage pregnancy, family violence, and incest. What is interesting is that their list paralleled the one drawn up by American psychologists, illustrating that the changes having an impact on families today are being felt worldwide. These changes also have a profound impact on our churches today.

It takes no prophet to predict there will be more hurting people, more psychologically scarred youth, and more dysfunctional families in the future of our congregations.[1] And this emerging phenomenon of desperate need calls for new ways of conducting ministry.

The need to reevaluate a congregation's ministry is apparent to many congregational leaders. A parish pastor writing to his congregation emphasized this point:

> The form of a church's ministry does change in ways related to its time and place in history. Just as we wouldn't think of having a Tupperware party in rural Namibia or a five hour worship service in our city, so we must recognize that as society changes so also do many of the ways in which ministry gets done.
>
> We tend to think of Western society as the hub of Christianity. Yet Western Europe is essentially agnostic, including Scandinavia and Germany, from whence many of us came! While this is not yet true of the United States, the trend is here too. (The most recent data puts about 20 percent of Americans active to somewhat active in practicing their faith and involved in the life of their church. In Sweden the percentages range between 1 and 3 percent; in England it is around 6 percent.)
>
> This trend (toward secularism) represents a profound change over what was the case in Western Society for hundreds of years. The church stood at the center of society and if society never fully embraced the Christian faith in practice at least the faith's concepts and practices were understood. Today's societal change is so significant that there is becoming wide-spread agreement that we now live in a "post–Christian" age. Yet most congregations plan their ministry as though nothing has changed.
>
> The massive changes occurring within Western Society have profound implications for the church. They force an reevaluation of the church's role and require greater clarity regarding its mission.[2]

Mission does not originate with a congregation. It has its origin in the heart of God. It is God's concern and love for a lost humanity that caused God to send his Son, Jesus Christ, in order that all who believe in him may have everlasting life. During his ministry on this earth, Christ expressed God's love and concern by the way he reached out with compassion to the marginalized, people possessed by demons, those disabled by disease, the lepers, those facing the death of a loved one, the powerless, and the blind.[3]

God's revolutionary mission which Christ made visible through his preaching, teaching, and healing, has been given to his church. The congregation's task, then, is to be clear about God's mission and to discern what God is doing *in* the community and wants to do *through* it. Though the method of ministry may change, the basic mission of the church does not change. It's responsibility is summed up in the words of the Great Commission—"Go and make disciples of all nations" (Matthew 28:18–20), and in the Great Commandment—"Love each other as I have loved you" (John 15:12).

THE CONGREGATION—DIVINE AND HUMAN

According to the Bible, a congregation is the body of Christ, with characteristics both human and divine. Its divine calling is to promulgate a message that has the power to bring about profound changes in the lives of people. Though human endeavor admittedly is involved in proclaiming this message, God's Spirit is the principal driving force. According to Scripture, the primary source of resistance to the work of a congregation centers in the spiritual hosts of wickedness (angels, principalities, and powers) found in the unseen world that surrounds us, a reality to which the apostle Paul refers. Yet the work of advancing Christ's kingdom remains in the hands of humans who are prone to err, and at times, to sin blatantly. A unique human and divine dialectic is inextricably intertwined in the life and work of a congregation.

Though conscious of the human and divine dialectic that characterizes the church, the focus of this book is primarily on the human aspect of Christ's church. Our attention centers on its organizational efforts to bring this gospel of redemption to people coping with a variety of needs. We know only too well that it is in carrying out this task of spreading the gospel that the frailties of human flesh become evident. Aspects of people's humanity often become embarrassingly apparent when a pastor or lay leader introduces a new hymn book, or the prospect of a building program, or a possible change in the Sunday morning schedule. At such times the warts of a congregation appear as these proposed innovations are resisted for puzzling reasons. Some members seem intent on leaving their heel marks in the sands of progress.

When I conducted my last annual meeting in the only congregation I ever served, an old gentleman stood up and with a toothless grin gave this accurate account of the role he had played in congregational meetings. He said, "I have opposed every change that has been presented, insisting that if we wait it will be cheaper. I have to admit that every change you have voted in has been a good one." With that he sat down with a broad smile on his face.

This often laughable and human side of congregational life stands in constant tension with its divine side, a side often ignored when seeking to effect meaningful changes. When considering needed changes, it is easy to give too little credence to the spiritual resources God provides. That is why a congregation's attention needs periodically to be drawn to the importance of relying primarily on what God can do.

An Hispanic congregation (United Church of Christ) in Brooklyn, New York, does just that. This church of two hundred members working in a high-risk area takes prayer very seriously. On Monday evening a prayer service called "Family Prayer" is held. Children and youth are encouraged to attend. About seventy-five come to this service. On Tuesday another prayer service is held from 10 A.M. until 12 noon for the elderly who will not risk coming out at night.

The human-divine dialectic being discussed here suggests the following. The Church of Jesus Christ must live in an organizational tension between its humanness—as seen in characteristics it holds in common with other organizations—and its uniqueness, derived from its transcendental dimension.[4] Through its use of prayer, the claiming of God's promises, and the witness of its members, the church can unleash a unique power in the battle with God's spiritual opposition. At the same time, the church can take seriously the doctrine of creation, which views discoveries of the social sciences as God-given aids congregations can use in coping with their humanness.

Pastor Rick Warren, in *The Purpose Driven Church,* presents observations that have crystallized for him into convictions about growing churches. Having been a student of such churches over a period of twenty years, he believes he has learned most from watching what God has done in the church he started, Saddleback Valley Church. He observes:

The Bible clearly teaches that God has given us a critical role to play in accomplishing His will on earth. Church growth is a partnership between God and man. Churches grow by the power of God through the skilled effort of people. Both elements, God's power and man's skilled effort, must be present.[5]

In the discussions on change and innovation that follow, special attention will be given to this unique calling and dialectic, a uniqueness that sets congregations apart from all other service organizations.

THE NEED FOR INNOVATION

Making changes in a congregation's traditional ministry usually means introducing innovations. Though change and innovation are not always one and the same thing, we will here refer to them interchangeably.

What is an innovation? A useful definition is offered by Sandra Hale and Mary Williams in *Managing Change.*[6] An innovation is:

• The application of new ideas in an old setting.
• The application of old ideas in a new setting.

It is obvious from this definition that a congregation may launch a service perceived as new and innovative even though it resembles what was done centuries before. An illustration of this is found in Kuenning's *The Rise and Fall of American Lutheran Pietism.* He reports that in the early 1800s, congregations were taking an active role in the peace and reform movements of its day. For instance, the movement to abolish human slavery was "far and away the overriding moral reform issue of the day. It was the 'question of questions.'"[7] The response of congregations to social hurts of their day may be identified as innovative. In like fashion, efforts to address current issues can be viewed as innovative even though they repeat something that has been done before. What is deemed innovative may be nothing more than responding to a new cycle of concerns that today's society has made prominent and urgent.

Starting with Individuals

It is useful to know that innovations adopted by church bodies in the 1800s often came to the attention of their leaders through individuals troubled by omissions in the church's ministry. For instance, it took impassioned and visionary individuals to awaken the conscience of church leaders to their responsibility for preaching the gospel in foreign lands. The position of the church had largely been, "If God wants the heathen saved, God will find a way to do it." But through the efforts of men like William Carey, David Livingston, John R. Mott, and others, denominations became involved in missionary endeavors of significant proportions.

The Sunday school movement was another innovation. It was started in England by Robert Raikes, who was troubled by the sight of homeless young people terrorizing the streets. The Sunday schools he established to take these young people off the streets on Sunday became eminently successful. Later this innovation was transplanted to American soil, where as a parachurch organization it spread like a prairie fire across the states. Though started outside the church as an independent movement, Sunday schools later were embraced by the organized church as part of its ongoing ministry.

The same thing happened with the youth organizations that spontaneously blossomed during the second half of the nineteenth century. Francis E. Clark, who introduced the Christian Endeavor in 1875, applied an organizational response to a compelling need and created an overwhelming response among young adults. The leaders of many denominations, however, actively opposed the adoption of this innovation in church life. The secretary for one national youth organization known as the Luther League Federation wrote in its secretarial record, "We look forward to the day when we have only the devil and not also our church fathers to fight." Though these youth organizations flourished outside the control and supervision of the church, they finally were adopted by the organized church at the turn of the century as a legitimate expression of a congregation's responsibility.

The history of the church is one of change. These changes, however, have been slow in coming, and for many individuals the church's resistance to needed change has been troubling. These individuals have lamented the fact that by the time a new ministry has been launched, contact has been lost with that segment of the population to be served. Hence, the need in our day is to develop within congregations a greater ability and readiness to act quickly.

Innovations Take Time

Developing a readiness to respond is important because introducing an innovation is usually a slow process. Take, for instance, the time it takes to introduce a new product to the public. The number of years between conception of a new product and its adoption in the marketplace is surprising. One study documented the time between development and adoption of forty-six inventions. It found that the number of years ranged from twenty-two years (adoption of television) to five years (adoption of the spinning jenny). The average number of years to launch these forty-six inventions was thirteen years.[8]

A similar study by Battelle Laboratories in 1973 reported that the time lag between conceiving the idea for ten products until their acceptance in the marketplace averaged nineteen years. Listed in sidebar 1.1 are the number of years involved for a few of the products in this study.

It takes time to launch innovations, even those as attractive as television or videotape recorders. Hence, a time lag can be expected for new programs a denomination or congregation wishes to introduce. Kennon Callahan, in *Twelve Steps to an Effective Church*, insists that a congregation wishing to develop a major program should plan on four to five years of development.[9]

This point is significant when considering how long a pastor or staff worker remains with a congregation. When a leader stays only two or three years, how much positive change can be accomplished?

SIDEBAR 1.1	
Time Lapsed from Conception to Adoption	
Hybrid corn	25 years
Heart pacemaker	32 years
Videotape recorder	6 years
Oral contraceptives	9 years
Green revolution-wheat	16 years

Many pastors have found that it takes longer than four or five years to launch an innovative program because of the resistance to their proposals from a substantial number of parishioners. For these pastors, many a good idea has "died a borning," and the people who might have been served by the innovative ministry have gone elsewhere. Of course, at times parishioners have valuable ideas for change that are resisted by pastors.

Learning How to Innovate

An ideal worth seeking is to learn how to introduce innovations in a way that over time will equip a congregation with a greater readiness to respond, a predisposition to act quickly when needs become apparent. Such a predisposition requires:

- an attitude of openness
- a listening stance
- a strong mission focus
- a motivation to improve what is being done
- a minimum of internal conflict

These are characteristics of congregations ready to respond to emerging needs.[10]

This readiness is a possibility for your congregation. There are approaches to innovation that can change attitudes and increase the responsiveness of members. The result will be a shortened time between seeing a need and launching a significant ministry.

Your congregation needs to become what business consultant Peter Senge, in *the Fifth Discipline*, calls a "learning organization," one that is "continually expanding its capacity to create its future." Such an approach involves a mental shift from seeing parts to seeing wholes, from seeing a few to seeing all members as active participants in reacting to the present to create the future.[11] Doing this may require a change in culture or a change in how your members are involved. It may require new forms of ministries.

THE EFFECTIVENESS OF A CHANGE PROCESS

Ronald Lippitt, a former professor at the University of Michigan and a nationally acclaimed expert in consulting with groups on institutional change, observed:

There seem to be two different incentives for making improvement efforts. One of these is to confront a problem (e.g., complaints from people, low morale, drop in quality of services, or drop in income). The second incentive or push toward improvement is to use an "image of potential" where one's focus is on how things could be better.[12]

Our emphasis in this book is on his second incentive—that of being motivated by a vision of what could be, thus focusing on possibilities.

Admittedly, it takes more than following a set of procedures to bring about change effectively. Also important is the skill of the facilitator, the support of the institution's top executive, and the attention given to follow-up activities. But assuming these basic considerations are in place, the change process presented here can be remarkably effective. Andrew Leonie, a pastor skilled in using an approach called Vision-to-Action,[13] developed by Shelby Andress in consultation with Lippitt, took a dying parochial school and brought it back to life.

Though the illustration that follows would ideally be of a congregation, it is being used because the parochial school was approached much like a congregation. The story shows how faculty and staff moved through seven distinct steps to bring about remarkable changes in their situation (see figure 1 on page 21).

Resurrecting a Dying School

While serving as pastor of a congregation at Corpus Christi, Texas, Leonie received an urgent call to take over the leadership of a residential high school academy that was ready to fold. His time would have to be divided between the two institutions.

The church-sponsored academy had a $400,000 debt; its student body had shrunk to sixty-nine students; the administration building had been condemned and needed to be reconstructed; and for eight years the roof on the dining room, gymnasium, and music building had leaked when it rained.

The visionary change approach used by Leonie resulted in the debt being paid off, the student enrollment reaching over two hundred, the administration building being restored, and a new roof being put over the other departments. The academy has become the pride of its community and the joy of its twenty-six teachers.

Conceptual Model of the Planning Process

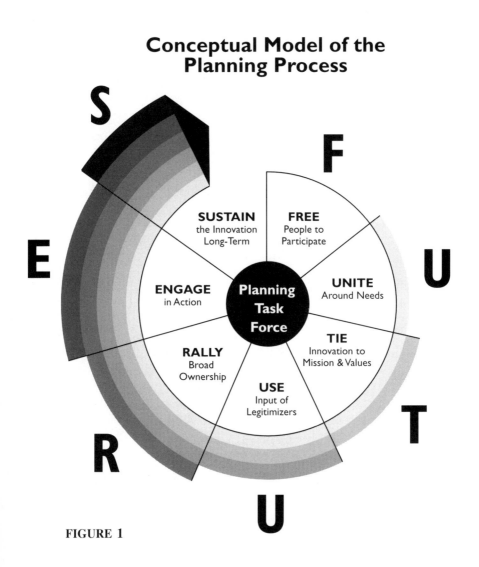

S

F

E

U

SUSTAIN
the Innovation
Long-Term

FREE
People to
Participate

ENGAGE
in Action

Planning
Task
Force

UNITE
Around Needs

RALLY
Broad
Ownership

TIE
Innovation to
Mission & Values

USE
Input of
Legitimizers

T

R

U

FIGURE 1

What did this man do? He followed seven steps that follow the conceptual model being presented in this book.

This conceptual model, based on data from the Innovation Study, presents the sequence of steps found useful in effecting needed change. As indicated by the diagram, once a step has been taken, its emphasis is continued while subsequent steps are taken. Thus all seven emphases are present when an innovation becomes part of the ongoing ministry of a congregation.

FREE PEOPLE TO PARTICIPATE. Leonie began by establishing a climate of openness and freedom among his faulty and staff during his opening orientation session. He spent his first two weeks helping his teachers see the need for an atmosphere of openness and caring. He wanted the faculty to be open to considering new approaches to parochial school education, to new ways of viewing students in need of discipline, ways that might differ from those typically at work in the Seventh-day Adventist Church.

During these days he asked them to face the question, Why a religious school? Facing that question in round-table discussions, the teachers came to see that one of their tasks was to teach young people who God is. Once seeing this God, the students could be helped to live to the ultimate what God had planned for them. This concept of religious education suggested rigorous academic standards and a school known as God's school.

With this basic stance that God is central, it was determined that the educational approach must have a strong moral base. If there is a lack of love, that needs to be changed. The guiding question became, "How can the curriculum and the way teachers teach convey love and grace?" If discipline is needed, it should be redemptive discipline. This kind of thinking was freeing for the teachers, who had felt obligated to enforce certain unwelcomed standards of the church.

By the end of the two weeks, the teachers felt free to affirm that their school should exist to fulfill the needs of the students and only secondarily the needs of the church. Thus the school and its program should be oriented both to Christ and the world in which the students must live.

UNITE AROUND NEEDS. Leonie's next step was to heighten the faculty's awareness of student needs by using the results of a national study of twelve thousand students in the church's parochial schools. Using the authority of solid data, he alerted the teachers to the needs and cries of the youth they serve. This resulted in conversations during that two-week period about what might be done in the school to meet these needs.

It was concluded that a curriculum should be designed to address the needs of students. The thinking was this: If the curriculum does not meet the needs of students, we will not be able to sell the school's program. Students will come to a private school because of its curriculum. In other words, curriculum is the school's primary marketing tool.

THE INNOVATION TO MISSION AND VALUES. Once the teachers were aware of the needs of the youth they were serving, they were free to formulate a revolutionary curriculum oriented to both academic and vocational preparation. The guiding question was, "How can our curriculum accomplish the mission we have for our students?" A track system was established whereby a student could select from twenty-two subjects that had a vocational aim and provided academic preparation. These tracks were based on interests identified by the students in a prior survey. Their statements of interest resulted in a nursing program for juniors and seniors to be completed seven months after graduation. Another program focused on making stained-glass windows, another on piloting an airplane, and another on the construction of stringed instruments. The resulting curriculum consisted of academic courses that included industrial training that could be pursued following graduation.

Significantly, it was agreed that faculty had the freedom to include reference to God and faith when teaching their subjects. Furthermore, it was determined it was unethical to enroll students who could not meet the academic standards of the school. Therefore, a special course was established to provide remedial training for those who needed it.

USE INPUT OF LEGITIMIZERS. Having arrived at an admittedly unique approach to a residential high school curriculum, special efforts were made to gain support for what was being proposed. To begin with, these plans were reported to the school board to gain its support. Because the school is partially supported by the conference treasury of the church, monthly reports were sent to the conference offices to keep that staff informed on what was being done. Furthermore, a questionnaire was sent to all pastors, parents, and leaders in the Texas Conference to gain their opinions regarding what was being done at the school. An accompanying letter showed how this new approach to education truly reflected the values of both family and church. The intent in all of this was to gain the support of the thought leaders and conference legitimizers by soliciting their reactions and advice regarding what was being initiated.

Interestingly, 60 percent of the pastors responded to the questionnaire. Of these, 97 percent said they liked the concept of a nursing program and 87 percent said they liked the concept of including vocational training with the academic offerings.

RALLY BROAD OWNERSHIP. A further step was taken to secure broad support by involving many different constituency groups. The school board was reorganized so its members would include persons from the Spanish population and representatives from all parts of the conference. Parents of students were invited to write personal letters to Leonie about how they felt about what was being done. Faculty members are invited to a luncheon every Monday for a time of sharing with Leonie. The emphasis of this gathering was on the idea "Look what God is doing for us." A prayer garden was built including a fish pond and private seating area for students to have special moments of prayer. A book of prayer requests is kept in the board room. Faculty and students can record prayer requests and answers to prayer in the book.

ENGAGE IN ACTION. The revolutionary curriculum was launched with a most favorable response from students, parents, community, and church members. It has been continued with improvements suggested by various constituencies.

SUSTAIN THE INNOVATION LONG-TERM. To ensure that the academic program would be improved each year, an elaborate feedback system was established. Committees were established to evaluate the programs; committee members included professionals and persons knowledgeable in areas related to specific subjects. At the end of the school year, a five-day evaluation was conducted with the faculty to review the past year and make improvements in what was to be offered the coming year.

This story shows how a change was extremely useful in resurrecting a dying school and restoring it to a significant place in God's mission. It is a remarkable story of how the teachers and staff developed a sensitivity to need and learned how to create innovative approaches that address these student needs. You will note how the story of Leonie's transformation of a school resembles the conceptual model being proposed here—a model summarized in the acronym FUTURES.

Just as the change process undergirded with much prayer brought about remarkable changes in a parochial school, the same can happen for a congregation. This is what took place for Central Christian Church in Decatur, Illinois. When the pastor came in 1973, he found a severely damaged congregation with the worship attendance of ninety-three, mostly older persons. The congregation grew to 2,600 members, and its outreach program covers a five-county area. It trains and places over 350 volunteers in more than fifty community agencies. A congregation's potential for change is unlimited because of its unique mission in a day rife with hurting people.

Innovation, a significant feature in the history of the church, is an essential element in the life of a congregation. It is the way a congregation can modify the nature of its ministries (not its message) to be more effective in reaching the outsider and those coping with distressing problems and circumstances. It is a way to become involved in what God is already doing.

Reflection:
Congregational Innovativeness

• In what ways has my congregation made alterations in its ministry in order to reach more hurting people?

• What are we doing in our congregation to increase people's anticipation of God's intervention?

• How long did it take from inception to adoption for our most recent congregational innovation to become established?

• Which steps in the FUTURES model do I tend to follow intuitively?

CHAPTER TWO

WHY DO CONGREGATIONS RESIST CHANGE?

> *"A fundamental principle of resistance is that people resist being forced to change."*
>
> —*Edward Glaser*

AS A CONGREGATIONAL LEADER, you may have been puzzled by the resistance to an innovation in ministry. For you the need being addressed was so obvious that you could not understand why there would be any opposition. You found yourself wondering, "Why is it so hard to effect a change that is so desperately needed? What causes some members to thwart needed progress in the kingdom of our Lord? What facilitates the making of needed change?"

OBSTACLES TO INNOVATION

Similar questions trouble heads of business, educational, and governmental institutions who likewise wish to effect significant changes in their organizations. They, too, find it difficult to introduce new ways of doing things and therefore wonder what it is that hinders or facilitates the needed change. The puzzling roadblocks to innovation encountered by leaders of any organization tend to fall under one of the following topics: (1) tradition, (2) personality, (3) ideology, (4) affiliation, and (5) demonic power.

Tradition

Every organization has its traditions, its unwritten norms, its way of doing things, some of which take on an almost sacred status. Though these traditions may have served well in the past, they now can be roadblocks to needed changes. Take, for instance, some of the procedures in Congress that have become accepted practice over the years. Today, many of these serve only to produce "gridlock." The siren call of special interest groups, the tendency to place party advancement in front of national interest, the concern of politicians to protect their political future have become enormous roadblocks to changes needed to advance our country's welfare.

Another illustration is found within institutions of higher learning. Their devotion to scholarly pursuits has created an anti-utilitarian stance. Research for bringing about changes that have a clear practical value typically evokes resistance within the academic world. It is not viewed as a scholarly pursuit.

Howard Davis was especially conscious of this attitude when serving as chief of the Mental Health Services Development Branch, a division of Mental Health Services. He wanted grants funded by his office to bring about significant changes for hurting people, and he was troubled by the resistance he encountered in academia to studies with a utilitarian purpose. He found research scholars who might present their findings in ways that would make them useful to policy makers and practitioners being downgraded when evaluated for promotion. Some even met contempt from their colleagues.

This reluctance to consider how knowledge might be applied in practical situations is found also among some seminary professors, who assume that once a student has knowledge on a given subject, he or she will know how to apply this knowledge in ministry. Hence, seminary subjects such as Christian education, homiletics, or youth ministry are deemed less appropriate for a scholarly enterprise. The resistance of faculty to including such "practical" subjects in their curriculum has long been a complaint of pastors in the field. They feel unprepared for situations requiring hands-on ministry with hurting people or unprepared to give leadership during times of congregational upheaval.

Obstacles to change can be seen in the New Testament story of Christ's ministry. Resistance to his message mounted as the scribes, priests, and Pharisees saw him violate their tradition—

their human ordinances, which had taken on a sacred quality. His daring to heal the sick and infirm on the Sabbath, his differing interpretation of Scripture, his disregard for some of their rules infuriated them. Their hatred and anger boiled over when they saw their religious establishment being threatened by Christ's popularity. Their resistance culminated in trying not only to get rid of him but also publicly to discredit him.

Congregations have long-established traditions that in the past may have served them well. But now some of these traditions may be serving as obstacles. That is why older churches find it much more difficult than newly established congregations to make changes in their approach to worship, to welcoming strangers, and to changes in governance. Granted, other factors are involved, but these will be considered in the sections that follow.[1]

Because this book presents research findings from a range of secular studies, it is important to note one of the significant findings from the Innovation Study: Congregations, because of their human dimension, have relatively the same organizational dynamics as secular organizations.[2] This suggests that when considering issues related to the human side of congregational life, we can profit from a range of research studies, whether congregationally based or not. In other words, insights from studies of secular organizations can be applied to congregations

Personality Differences

People vary tremendously in their acceptance of any change. This fact has been studied carefully by Everett Rogers and reported in his classic, *Diffusion of Innovations*. In his book, Rogers classifies adopters of an innovation on the basis of a personality characteristic he calls "innovativeness."[3] Figure 2.1 presents his classification,[4] one that has been tested through hundreds of studies. The percentages are estimates.

INNOVATORS. These are the venturesome ones who are eager to try new ideas. Every congregation has a few such people. Innovators in the life of the denomination often come from outside its administrative structure. Here one only needs to think of William Carey, who launched the idea of foreign missions; Robert Raikes, who started the Sunday school movement; Francis E. Clark,

Innovativeness Categories

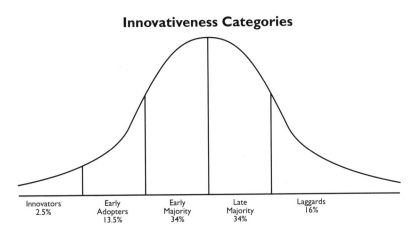

FIGURE 2.1

Relationship of Independent Variables to Innovativeness

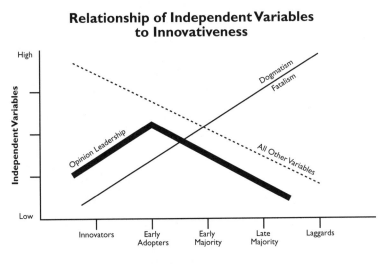

ADOPTER CATEGORIES

Opinion leadership tends to characterize early adopters whereas dogmatic and black-and-white thinking tends to characterize laggards. All other variables such as social status, education, and broad experience are most likely to characterize innovators and early adopters and not the late majority and laggards.

FIGURE 2.2

who made Christian Endeavor the harbinger of church youth organizations; and Billy Graham, who has succeeded in giving reality to John R. Mott's dream of a world evangelism movement. All were visionaries who established movements outside the denomination that later were embraced and made part of church life.

When speaking of innovators, one is reminded of Paul and Barnabas, who took the risk of taking the gospel to the Gentiles and receiving them as full brothers and sisters in the faith, even though faced with opposition.

> Then Paul and Barnabas answered [the Jews] boldly: "We had to speak the word of God to you first. Since you reject it and do not consider yourselves worthy of eternal life, we now turn to the Gentiles. For this is what the Lord has commanded us: 'I have made you a light for the Gentiles, that you may bring salvation to the ends of the earth'" (Acts 13:46–47).

According to Rogers the interest of innovators leads them out of a local circle of peer networks and into more cosmopolitan social relationships.[5] They will pursue a new idea even though it may be untried, daring, or risky. For that reason innovators are able to start a new business based on an invention or new procedure they have championed. Unfortunately, the innovator is less able to structure and organize in ways needed to institutionalize an innovation. As a result one commonly hears of innovators who have started a new and visionary enterprise being replaced by a person better able to administrate. Figure 2.1 shows only 2.5 percent of the people in an organization, including a congregation, will be innovators. It should also be noted (see figure 2.2) that innovators do not rank high in opinion leadership. Some people find it hard to take them seriously.

EARLY ADOPTERS. The early adopter, according to Rogers, is the one considered by many as "the person to check with before using or acting on a new idea." This person is respected by his or her peers and frequently serves in a leadership role. Studies of early adopters show them to have more years of education than later adopters, more likely to be literate, to show greater upward mobility, and to have a higher social status. In a study to identify which university officials were most likely to adopt a new communication technology, Rogers found early adopters, when compared with later adopters, exhibit greater empathy (the ability to project oneself into the role of another person), less dogmatism, more rationality, and a greater ability to deal with abstraction.[6]

Without question, early adopters are the forward thinking pastors, youth ministers, directors of Christian education, and lay leaders who early on have a vision for how a new idea might work in their parish. They are usually people who have inspired trust by the way they approach people. An example from the early church is James the brother of Jesus, who as head of the Jerusalem church led the way to accepting Gentiles into the church. His acceptance prompted others to follow his lead (Acts 15:19–21).

EARLY MAJORITY. Though these people seldom hold leadership positions, they adopt new ideas sooner than the average member of a social system. They will deliberate longer than the innovator or early adopter before accepting a new idea but not because they are resistant to an idea. They are like those described by Alexander Pope in 1711: "Be not the first by whom the new are tried, nor the last to lay the old aside."[7] These people are the deliberate ones. They need to hear all sides of a proposed change and then be given time to ponder their decision.

LATE MAJORITY. These people tend to approach a new idea with skepticism and caution. They usually will not agree to an innovation until most of the others in their group have agreed to it. Pressure from their peers is usually needed to motivate them to cast a favorable vote. They constitute a substantial part of a congregation's membership (see figure 2.1). They are likely to drag their feet when asked to support a significant alteration in how things are done.

A classic example can be found in Peter, who had initially taken a lead in accepting the Gentiles. But later we see him backpedaling until his peer in ministry, Paul, directly confronted him. Peter had difficulty with change because he allowed "laggards" to influence him (Galatians 2:11–13).

LAGGARDS. These are the last ones in a social system to adopt an innovation. Though possessing little or no opinion leadership, their 16 percent size constitutes a significant group. Although they seldom occupy an elected position or speak up in an assembly to voice a dissenting opinion, they will still make themselves heard.

These people will express their resistance in the parking lot, or over a social coffee, or when talking to a friend on the phone.

Laggards tend to be suspicious of both innovations and change agents. Their attention is fixed on the rearview mirror. One reason for their reticence to consider anything new centers in their limited resources. Laggards typically have the least education and the least exposure to new ideas or situations. They are the most likely of all groups to favor doctrinaire, black-and-white positions. Dogmatism and fatalism are two characteristics strongly associated with laggards. They favor a hold-the-line stance in all aspects of life.

In the Jerusalem council situation, the laggards might be compared to the Pharisees, who insisted that Gentile Christians live by the laws of Moses, including those requiring circumcision. Their dogmatic views prevented them from grasping the concept of grace. Instead, they could accept only the legalistic positions of the past. Evidence of their fixed position is reflected in what they were teaching. "Unless you are circumcised, according to the custom taught by Moses, you cannot be saved" (Acts 15:1).

My friend Paul Krentz writes:

> My observation is that laggards are often "'pioneer land rights" members. In our church, some are charter members from twenty-five years ago who no longer want to hold elected or appointed positions. But they still expect to be opinion setters by virtue of their pioneer role. They are very "economics driven." Their first question is, "How can we expect to afford this?" When expressing their concerns they say, "Some of us have been talking" or "I have heard some saying" to give credence to their position. Leaders often get caught emotionally by these kind of comments even though the "we" or the "they" might be only two or three people.[8]

This portion of a congregation's membership includes a group of adults who are hard to convince. When anything new is introduced, they raise questions such as the following:

- Who originated this idea?
- What do others think about it?
- How will it affect my area of responsibility?

Though these questions seem harmless and even reasonable, they do identify people who are hard to convince and likely to drag their feet. Often the people asking these questions are the ones who always want additional information. No matter how much information is given, it is never enough.

A second attitude of resistance is found in people who hold an honest preference for the status quo. They are people who psychologically resist anything new, and they know it. When asked in our survey about their reaction to an innovation, these people candidly agreed to the following:

- I feel uneasy if it seems "too new."
- I prefer staying with what we are doing.
- I prefer to be involved only partially in something new.
- I will feel that something is being railroaded through.

The items, which form a distinct cluster, describe the thinking of people in every congregation who frankly hesitate to become involved in anything new. They are content with current approaches and present horizons. Their resistance to innovation, though mild, is nevertheless sufficient to slow a congregation's response to any proposal involving a significant change.

These people need to be taken into consideration, for in some cases their resistance is not obstinacy or bull-headedness but a true expression of a personality temperament. Jerome Kagan, a developmental psychologist at Harvard University, has identified a dimension of temperament, ranging from timidity to boldness, that is due to a pattern of brain activity. Persons born with a neurochemistry that is easily aroused to fearfulness tend to avoid the unfamiliar, shy away from uncertainty, and suffer anxiety. Other people have a nervous system that is calibrated to a much higher threshold of arousal and as a result tend to be much more outgoing, eager to explore new places and meet new people.[9]

Obstacles to change, however, involve more than the differing personalities of people. A significant obstacle is found also in the values and beliefs that form an individual's worldview.

Ideology

The Minneapolis *Star Tribune* (April 15, 1996) carried an article about the first female president of the National Rifle Association,

Marion Hammer. Surrounded by pictures of grinning grandchildren this woman, in amazing disregard of the tragedies foisted on society by the misuse of guns, said, "It is truly not guns that kill people. Individuals do." Having disposed of the problem with this statement, she insisted that the solution to gun violence is not gun control but to "get rid of all liberals." Her commitment was to overturn federal legislation that outlawed assault weapons.

What leads such persons to hold positions viewed negatively by the vast majority of Americans? The answer lies in the person's ideological stance. From her perspective, it is right to resist any innovation that would restrict, even in a modest way, the possession of firearms.

In *Megatrends*, John Naisbitt, a social forecaster and business consultant, makes the point that people's receptivity to ideas is powerfully influenced by where they live. Each area of our country tends to foster a certain view of life that could be plotted on a conservative-liberal continuum. Naisbitt contends that most of the social inventions in the United States have occurred in five states that he calls bellwether states. He singles out California as a trend setter followed by Florida, Washington, Colorado, and Connecticut. Changes in lifestyle, political action, legislation, and educational standards have tended to rise first in these states. He assumes a geographical area tends to cultivate a mind-set that is reflected in the way its citizenry respond to new proposals.

In the past we were conscious of the deeply entrenched attitudes of Southerners toward African Americans. Today we are hear about the ready-to-fight convictions of ranchers in the West toward the federal government. Some of the ideas held by these "freedom fighters" regarding government plots to erase their freedom, illustrate "groupthink," being captive to the prevailing opinion of a community, area, or group of people. Those who are part of groupthink tend to employ selective perception. They interpret information in a way consistent with their prior attitudes and experience. This ability to perceive information selectively makes it possible for some to ardently believe that the United Nations is planning to invade the United States and impose a police state.

Another facet of groupthink is selective exposure. Those involved in this stance toward life, listen to or read only those messages that fit their opinion. Closely related to this mentality is selective retention, the tendency to remember only those communications that are consistent with ones prior attitudes and experiences.[10]

A culture or community can program the subconscious of its people in ways that powerfully inclines them to accept or reject certain ideas. One needs only think of how different people's attitudes toward social change are in countries as dissimilar as Iran, China, Israel, and Russia.

Affiliation

An ideological stance, however, is also powerfully shaped by one's organizational affiliations. A striking illustration of this is found in Search Institute's study of the values and beliefs of legislators in the Ninety-sixth Congress. Two factors accounted for most of the differences in their voting record. One was the person's system of values and belief and the other was the person's political affiliation. These two factors accounted for as much as 70 percent of the variance on some of their publicly recorded votes.[11] Rarely does one find such a high percentage of variance being accounted for when attempting to identify the main contributors to a given action.

People's ideological stance is obviously shaped by their political and religious affiliations. We are not surprised to see people oppose innovations in conflict with their organization's philosophy. Think of the widespread resistance of Roman Catholics to abortion. This political innovation on the American scene is strongly opposed by people who themselves may otherwise be early adopters. They are in militant opposition because the innovation violates values and beliefs they share with their church.

Consider the highly significant role of religion in the world today. In a book edited by Douglas Johnson and Cynthia Sampson, *Religion: The Missing Dimension of Statecraft*, we see how religion can cause conflict and resolve it. The church can support an oppressive elite, as the Catholic church did during much of Filipino history and the Dutch Reformed Church during South Africa's years of apartheid. But in both cases, when these churches underwent a dramatic transformation, they became major forces for change. The Catholic Church successfully opposed President Ferdinand Marcos and became instrumental in removing him from power. The Dutch Reformed Church, through its theologian

Willie Janker, confessed the sin of justifying apartheid. Desmond Tutu accepted this apology on behalf of the blacks to bring about a new openness and spirit of reconciliation that powerfully influenced Fredrik W. de Klerk.[12]

Though a religious faith can lead a person to resist innovation, even to the point of divisiveness and intolerance, it can also be a positive factor in promoting needed change. Frank Buchman, founder of Moral Rearmament, was successful in bringing the French and Germans together during the years 1946 to 1950. He was committed to changing nations and the world. He believed that for this to happen the consciousness of individuals must first change.[13] Hence, his approach and that of his Oxford Group, headquartered in Caux, Switzerland, was to bring people together and convince them to listen to each other.

The nature of one's religious stance, it must be added, is a significant element in determining people's reaction to a new idea. This became strikingly evident in Search Institute's monumental project, A Study of Generations, which showed that people's concept of Christianity tends to be either gospel-oriented or law-oriented.

Law-oriented people cannot tolerate change. They have a need for religious absolutism; they are prejudiced, threatened by people different from themselves, and self-seeking in their relation to religion; and basically hold to a salvation by works. Such law-oriented persons are found in every denomination and congregation and will be among those who resist the introduction of new ministries.

Sociologist Arthur Johnson, University of Minnesota, studied those having either a law or gospel orientation to the Christian faith. In doing so, he came up with four different types of people. (1) He found that those high on gospel and low on law tend to be progressive, interested in education, supporters of colleges, and ready to help found new organizations. (2) The ones high on law and high on gospel tend to be dutiful people whom you can always count on to support their congregation but who are likely to resist change. (3) Those low on gospel but high on law tend to be prejudiced, self-centered, condemnatory, and opposed to helping people in need. (4) Those low on both of these qualities tend to be secular and faddish in what they support. Clearly, it is the gospel-oriented members who will evidence a readiness to act when new forms of ministry are needed.

Another factor in organizational affiliation influences people's response to innovations. It has to do with organizational structure. Organizations that are highly structured foster a competitive atmosphere that encourages questions such as the following whenever anything new is proposed: How will it affect my place in the organization? To what degree will it increase my workload?

This sensitivity surfaced in the Innovation Study when we asked respondents how they react to proposed innovations. A certain percentage answered: I would . . .

- wonder if the new assignments will mean a higher level of responsibility for me.
  - think of the added load it will place on our workers.
  - wonder if a criticism of our current efforts is implied.
  - be suspicious of it if I distrust the presenter.
  - think of what must be given up if we adopt it.
  - be uneasy if I think it could fail.

This fear of extra work or loss of turf surfaced as a mild but real form of resistance, one that could be expected in a highly organized group. Sometimes this resistance is a legitimate one, fueled by excessive demands on time and energy. This is a real consideration for service institutions where task always exceeds personnel time. An innovation may not be welcomed simply because the plates of all involved are too full and anything more is "too much" for staff and volunteers. When trying to answer the question "Why is it so hard to effect change?" one comes to realize that one is involved with a "dynamic complexity."[14] People influenced by systems that subtly shape their thinking and actions vary considerably in how they will respond to an innovation.

Demonic Power

Because congregations are both human and divine institutions, they face an added dimension of resistance that is spiritual in nature. The opposition is found in obstacles that contemporary century Western society tends to exclude from ordinary conversation. As Walter Wink says in *Unmasking the Powers*, "Angels, spirits, principalities, powers, gods, Satan—these along with other spiritual realities, are the unmentionables of our culture."[15]

The apostle Paul is very clear in his letters that God's faithful are involved in a battle against spiritual hosts of wickedness in heavenly places. We could interpret this to mean that sometimes the resistance encountered by a congregation is the demonic. Spiritual beings can resist a congregation's ministry in a real way, though obviously not all resistance to change is demonic. But this phenomenon of battling spiritual hosts of wickedness is one aspect of a congregation's uniqueness. As Paul wrote: "For our struggle is not against flesh and blood, but against the rulers, against the authorities, against the powers of this dark world and against the spiritual forces of evil in the heavenly realms" (Ephesians 6:12).

Unless a congregation recognizes its uniqueness and realizes that it is more than a human organization, we might say it is not the church. For Richard Hutcheson, author of *Wheel within the Wheel,* the uniqueness of the church is the active presence of the Holy Spirit:

> The unique mark of the church—which sets it apart from all other organizations—is the gift of the Holy Spirit. In the classic phrase of John Calvin, echoed both by Jürgen Moltmann and Hans Kung, the church is the "creation of the Spirit." The power of its members is the power of the Holy Spirit moving among them and all activity of the church (including the way it operates as an organization) which seeks to express God's purposes must be understood in this light."[16]

CHANGE TAKES TIME

The issue of resistance to change with which we are dealing has been known to writers down through the ages. In 1513, Niccolo Machiavelli wrote in *The Prince:*

> There is nothing more difficult to plan, more doubtful of success, nor more dangerous to manage than the creation of a new order of things. Whenever his enemies have occasion to attack the innovator they do so with the passion of partisans, while the others defend him sluggishly so that the innovator and his party alike are vulnerable.[17]

We cannot assume that advantageous innovations will sell themselves or that the world will beat a path to the door of a person who builds a better mousetrap.[18] A classic example of this is found in the length of time it took for the British Navy to act on information regarding the prevention of scurvy, the worst killer of the world's sailors. Vasco de Gama lost 100 of his men to scurvy from his crew of 160 who sailed with him around the Cape of Good Hope in 1497. In 1601, an English captain, James Lancaster, tested the effectiveness of lemon juice to prevent scurvy by giving three teaspoonfuls every day to sailors on the largest of his four ships. Those on the three smaller ships received none. Most of those on his largest ship remained healthy, while 110 of the 178 on the other three ships died of scurvy.

In 1747 a British Navy physician who knew of Lancaster's results carried out further experiments on the effects of citrus fruits. His experiment provided solid evidence regarding the ability of citrus fruits to combat scurvy. But it was not until 1795 that the British Navy adopted this innovation for all sailors on long sea voyages. Once the innovation was adopted, scurvy was immediately wiped out.[19]

This illustration gives dramatic evidence that the world does not beat a path to the builder of a better mousetrap. In every group there are puzzling roadblocks that keep people from adopting procedures known to be superior to those being used. Some of these roadblocks to innovation might be at work in your congregation. For that reason it would be useful for you as congregational leader to identify the most formidable ones. Once identified, they could be taken into consideration when preparing to make a needed change.

Reflection:
Obstacles Within My Congregation

Which of the following obstacles might seriously impede the making of needed change within my congregation?

- Long established traditions, now sacred, that resist change.
- A disproportionate number of late majority and laggard-type people.

• Members being influenced by attitudes dominating this part of the country.

• Institutional affiliations that encourage a groupthink mentality.

• A destructive evil that tears families apart and divides people in our congregation and community.

The thesis of this book is that obstacles such as these can be overcome by using task forces and the change process identified in the FUTURES model. When adequate time is allowed and resistance normal to any organization is taken into account, we can expect to see growth and development. The key to innovative activity, however, centers in the work of dedicated task forces, an aspect of innovation to be discussed in the next chapter.

CHAPTER THREE

THE KEY TO INNOVATION: TASK FORCES

"A small, cohesive change group within an organization is necessary to provide leadership in the change process. This group needs a leader who continuously pushes for change and attempts to keep the group organized and its morale high. This change group must be a cohesive group of interacting and committed people."

—G. W. Fairweather

THIS CHAPTER DOES NOT DENY the value of standing committees within a congregation. Many have served well in the past and may yet be needed to maintain a congregation's existing program. In one congregation where I conducted a Vision-to-Action workshop, the pastor concluded that two of the standing committees were better suited to serve as task forces than newly formed groups. She saw them as best able to bring about the desired innovations.

Though exceptions can be cited, I believe task forces are the key to innovation. The reason is this: A standing committee or board usually consists of members who have been asked to stand for election to a position in the congregation. The question they usually ask is, "What is involved?" The answer usually given is, "This committee meets once a month and is responsible for this area of congregational life." So the persons in question meet once a month to help maintain the programs related to their area of responsibility.

Members of a standing committee tend to see themselves as part of a policy-forming group whose focus is on matters inside the church. They generally see their job as protecting what is already in place. Though adequate for maintenance, standing committees are not geared for the long-range, thoughtful efforts required for quality, lasting innovations. Often the most exciting things happening in a congregation have been initiated outside a standing committee.

A significant innovation can require as much as three years or more to be established in a congregation. For it to become a lasting innovation, steps need to be followed that are similar to those outlined in our FUTURES model. These steps include:

- Freeing people to participate in a spontaneous way.
- Uniting people around an awareness of need.
- Tying the proposed innovations to the congregation's mission.
- Using the input of legitimizers and thus gaining their suport.
- Rallying broad ownership of all groups impacted by the innovation.
- Engaging people in testing the innovation on a trial basis.
- Sustaining the innovation long-term by evaluation and fine-tuning.

Planning consultant Kennon Callahan, in *Effective Church Leadership,* underscores the need for change groups. He calls for the creation of mission teams instead of committees. His attitude toward the traditional committee system is reflected in this statement: "The more committees, the less mission. The fewer committees, the more mission."[1] He adds, "A cause needs a leader not a committee." Therefore, the pastor should seek out a leader whose longings and competencies are a match for the cause. The leader then can form a team or task force drawing on the type and number deemed necessary to carry out the mission.

Peter Senge, of the Massachusetts Institute of Technology, also makes a similar case for the importance of developing teams that can translate visions into reality. He notes that in the realm of business, teams (whether management teams, product development teams, or cross-functional task forces) are making almost all the important decisions in the company. They translate individual decisions into action. They are becoming the key learning unit in an organization.

Business consultant Robert Waterman, coauthor of *In Search of Excellence,* is also convinced that successful innovation requires the effective use of problem-solving groups (tasks forces) operating outside the normal bureaucracy. His twenty-five years in management consulting have convinced him that the real action in an organization occurs outside " the proper channels." A bureaucracy is not geared for coping with change. Therefore he has written a book that focuses on what he calls "the most common, sturdy, and visible ad hoc form- the task force or project team." The title of his book is *Adhocracy—The Power to Change.* For him, a well-run task force has several attributes that make it ideal for effecting change.

First, a task force is designed to make change happen. It solves one of the most common organizational problems: big ideas but lousy implementation. Second, task force members eventually become proponents; that is, they tell others about what was agreed should be done and why an innovation is important. And third, and most importantly, they provide the very best thinking because it is their only consideration and task (in contrast to standing committees, which have a broad area of responsibility).[2]

Waterman does not think the formal structure of a bureaucracy should be eliminated in favor of task forces but that the two should coexist. He sees one as effective in maintaining the present program and the other as effective in launching innovative programs.

This dual approach of Waterman is certainly best suited for congregations whose formal structure is already well established and for whom efforts to eliminate committees and boards would precipitate a revolution. A good start is to begin with two or three task forces (a pilot effort) that will give the pastor or other leader time and experience in serving as teacher and coach. Once task forces have become learning teams, they will have added a creative dimension to your congregation.

The task force idea is used in education as well as in business or congregation. Japanese schools, for instance, use it to good advantage. Classes there are divided into teams, each with a leader. The team is responsible for the performance of all students in the group. The leader may call group members after school to make sure assignments are well understood. If not, the leader might meet the student before class. The burden of learning is on the group of students and not the teacher. Students, not the parents or teachers, help each other keep up with the lesson.

TASKS THAT REQUIRE TASK FORCES

Two types of tasks require that teams meet together over time with one objective in mind. One type, familiar to everyone, relates to special tasks in the life of a congregation that are outside the committee system. Here we are thinking of a building or call committee. The other type of task is creative, one designed to bring into being a congregation's visions, ministries that as yet do not exist.

Special Tasks

People may be elected at a business meeting to serve on a building committee. Their task is to spearhead efforts to implement the dream of a new church or an extensive addition.

This team of people is involved in a major innovation. Even though the project has been authorized at a church business meeting, it cannot be assumed that everyone in the congregation is aware of the decision, that all are in favor of it, or that all will give what is needed if a building fund drive becomes necessary. Their task, a complex one, involves developing a vision of what can be and then trying to bring the congregation along to support the effort.

The importance of involving the congregation is what the chairman of a building committee in a large Minneapolis congregation discovered several years ago. He had not considered the need for a change process. His committee, a good one, worked diligently and hard to determine what they thought the congregation needed in a new sanctuary and educational unit. They drew up plans that reflected their thinking and then determined the cost. When their proposal was suddenly thrust upon the members for congregational authorization, the chairman could hardly believe the negative reaction. Members, feeling no ownership in what was proposed, voted against the project. The task force had failed to gain the participation of members when going through the various normal steps of a building project

Two years later his committee again addressed the need for additional buildings but this time took care to involve the congregation using the steps in our FUTURES model. This time the reaction of members was very different. Today this congregation enjoys the expanded ministry made available through the addition of a new sanctuary and educational unit.

Another important task force is the call committee, chosen again at the congregational business meeting to represent the entire membership. These people are charged with the important task of identifying criteria, interviewing candidates, and recommending a person who might become the next pastor. Like the building committee, these people can accomplish their task more effectively if they use a planning process that transforms the team into a learning unit.

Building committees, call committees, and mission statement committees classify as task forces. They are charged with a specific task requiring thought, time, and a planning process.

Visionary Tasks

In addition to the functions mentioned above, your congregation needs task forces that are visionary in their efforts, that are intent on bringing about dreams members have for their congregation. By way of illustration, here are four visions that were given the highest priority rating of importance by forty-two members of First Lutheran Church in Duluth, Minnesota.

Four Congregational Visions

These people had each written scenarios describing what would please them very much if they could see it happening three years hence. Each vision given below is a composite of all written scenarios that focused on the same desired outcome.

1. Goal-Oriented Christian Education

• We see teachers involved in a monthly Bible study that focuses on such questions as: "What kind of experience do we want for the children?" "What outcomes do we pray might be realized?" and "How do we foster such outcomes?"

• The nursery is more than baby-sitting; it is a time when faith is introduced.

• Parents are involved to help with singing and creative expression.

• Children and parents come to know each other by name.

• Older children and youth learn why and how the Bible and its stories can be important in their lives.

• There is a strong emphasis on going beyond factual information to knowing how Scripture applies to me, to knowing Jesus Christ as friend and Savior.

• Confirmation has three levels, for those with no faith background, for those with some, and for those with much.

2. Accent on Scripture

• We see a sustained effort to engage members in the use of their Bible, an effort so appealing to men that they become leaders in this emphasis.

• Fifty percent of the congregation's men are now involved in some form of Bible study.

• Different levels of study are offered, and groups are established for everyone from those with no background to those who can dig into a book in the Bible.

• People bring their Bibles to church and use them.

• Bible stories are a focal part of family devotions.

• Youth act out lessons learned from the Bible and apply them to life situations.

3. Intentional Outreach to the Community

• Youth and adults are working together in an intentional outreach to the community through such groups as Women's Transitional Housing, Habitat for Humanity, and so forth.

• The programs they sponsor are characterized by an openness to people's concerns and lifestyles while being characteristically Bible-based, loving, and forgiving.

• Members learn as their lives are blessed through the exchange.

• The church building is open for programs such as tutoring, matching families for mutual-support, and a drop-in center.

4. Family Friendly Worship Service

• We see a lively family service where people of all ages play an active role in the service as readers, ushers, singers, greeters, and so forth.

• Movement is welcomed, participation is viewed as educational, and the service has an affective impact that touches the hearts of people.

• A wide variety of music with a contemporary flavor is used.

• If the service is held in an afternoon or evening, it is followed by a meal or snack, Bible study, or fun activities.

As is evident from reading each vision, several innovations will be needed before each vision becomes a reality. With each innovation, the congregation can expect an incremental gain toward achieving the vision, gains people can see and celebrate.

FORMING A TASK FORCE

A small, cohesive change group within an organization is necessary to provide leadership in the change process. This change group, or task force, needs a leader who continuously pushes for the desired change and attempts to keep the group organized and its morale high. This change group must be a cohesive team of committed people.

The task force should be small (no more than eight), including people from important subgroups, people of skill and knowledge, and people who are compatible. Robert Waterman has observed that during the span of his twenty-five years in consulting, the best teams have had between three and seven members. An important quality for this group is their toughness in holding unto a vision and persevering even when their efforts are not immediately rewarded.

A useful tool in helping a task force become organized is the Action Plan Worksheet I (on page 48).

ACTION PLAN—Worksheet I

Desired Outcome:

	KEY CONSIDERATIONS	ACTION STEPS	PERSONS RESPONSIBLE	WHEN?
Task Force	How can we best function as a Task Force to see our outcome achieved?	How often should we meet and where?	Who will serve as convener? Who will serve as documenter?	By what dates?
Feedback	How shall we evaluate what is launched?	How shall we decide on needed improvements?	Who is responsible to do what?	When?
Prayer	How can we undergird our efforts with prayer and a greater reliance on God's help?	Steps we might take:	Who is responsible to do what?	

Task Force Members:

Date:

The Leader's Role

Developing task forces to nurture a creative edge in your congregation calls for a new leadership role for the pastor. One that is especially appropriate is the role of teacher. As teacher, the pastor can help a task force see the big picture and within that establish a focus for their efforts. As teacher, the pastor can also help a group function as a group, follow change procedures, and systematically plan. (This applies also to policy-making groups such as your church council.)

According to Peter Senge, one of the pastor's roles is to *inspire* (literally, "to breathe life into") the vision of becoming a learning organization. This includes helping each task force master the practices of dialogue and discussion, which they will need to seek, a free and creative exploration of complex and subtle issues. Members must learn how to listen to each other and exchange ideas. If you are a pastor, your job is to help get things started but never to lead the task force. Make yourself available the first time they meet and help them structure their task. Your role is to act as coach, to encourage task force members to think boldly, and to offer help when needed.

A helpful beginning is to assist the group in arriving at a clear statement of their desired outcome, what they wish will happen as a result of their vision becoming a reality. Below are illustrations of such outcome statements. They were formulated by the task forces of First Lutheran Church in Duluth as their initial step in bringing reality to the four visions found on pages 52 and 53.

Desired Outcomes of the Four Visions

1. Goal-Oriented Christian Education. A comprehensive Christian education program for all members that develops a personal faith in Christ, knowledge of Scripture, and the application of faith to daily life.

2. Accent on Scripture. A sustained and creative involvement of all in some form of Bible study.

3. Intentional Outreach to the Community. Growth in faith and Christian witness through a program that links spiritual, physical, and emotional needs of the greater community with the gifts and talents of our church.

4. Family-Friendly Worship. A worship service where all ages feel a sense of belonging while sharing the joy of God's presence.

A simple statement of desired outcome, such as these, enables a task force to know its purpose. It helps task force members think about which innovations are needed to bring about their hoped-for outcome. An innovation may be a service, a plan, an event, a program, or procedure that contributes in some way to the realization of the vision.

Becoming a Learning Team

Because a task force must function over time and think insightfully about complex issues, it can become a microcosm for learning within the congregation. Two facets of development were shown in our study to be important predictors of the likelihood of task force success.

A SENSE OF TEAM. One of the most rewarding aspects of task force activity is the sense of meaning that comes from being part of something significant. People talk about being part of something larger than themselves, of being connected, of being generative.

Peter Senge speaks of teams, in which during the process of an activity people learn to trust each other, complement each other's strengths, seek common goals that are larger than personal goals, and produce extraordinary results.[3] This is the ideal one seeks not only because of what is accomplished but because of what it establishes in the congregation and the satisfaction it gives participants. It yields feelings such as those described by items from the Innovation Study that formed the cluster shown in sidebar 3.1. (The clusters identified in this book are called scales because the items also serve as a measure of the construct described in each title.)

SIDEBAR 3.1
Scale 1: Sense of Team
(Members identify with group and mission)

- I feel a part of our group.
- I feel satisfied with opportunities given me to use my abilities.
- I know what I am supposed to be doing in my role in my group.
- I enjoy my work here.

The apostle Paul in his first letter to the Corinthians emphasized the idea of teamwork when he described a congregation. He portrayed it as a body: "Now the body is not made up of one part but of many. . . . There are many parts, but one body. If one part suffers, every part suffers with it; if one part is honored, every part rejoices with it" (1 Corinthians 12:14, 20, 26).

This feeling of being a part of a team is enhanced by the exchange of information that lets people know the job they are doing is going well or needs to be modified in some way. Feedback of this sort is the lifeblood of an organization because it makes everyone feel a part of the system, helping to carry out an important part of the enterprise.[4]

PRIDE IN ACCOMPLISHMENT. As members learn how to face problems, initiate solutions, and become innovative in programming, they experience a sense of legitimate pride and satisfaction.

I remember the Sunday when an adult forum at our congregation faced the issue of homeless families in our community. We learned there were twice as many homeless families in our community as there were places they could live. Spurred by feelings of concern, a task force of eight people began addressing the problem to see what our congregation could do. After hundreds of phone calls and visits to social service agencies, the task force came to understand the complexity of the problem and the technical requirements involved in various solutions. But these eight stuck with it until they had arrived at an innovative approach to transitional housing that was doable. The plan they developed included housing and professional counseling over a period of two years to help single mothers become established and financially self-sufficient while caring for their children. It was a source of satisfaction and pride for all concerned, not least the task force, to see an exemplary program in place providing homes for six or more families each year.

The cluster of items from the Innovation Study that describe this sense of pride and identify the innovative skills members have acquired,[5] are listed in sidebar 3.2.

Agreeing on Innovations

Once an agenda is tentatively established for the next several years, the task force can focus on the first innovation—one chosen because it is less demanding to inaugurate and because it will bring visible results in a relatively short time. Change is best seen as a process of small wins. When leaders deliberately cultivate a strategy of small wins they make it easier of people to go along with their requests.[6]

Below are innovations the four task forces at First Lutheran Church chose for their beginning efforts.

1. Goal-Oriented Christian Education

Innovation 1: Develop a plan for an integrated, coordinated Christian education program from birth to death, based on human and faith development stages.

Innovation 2: Develop a plan to involve parents in children's Christian education classes, groups, and activities.

2. Accent on Scripture

Innovation 1: Make Bibles available in pews for adults and children and as a gift to all new members.

Innovation 2: Offer Bible study for all levels of interest. Schedule Bible studies at varying times and places to be taught by both clergy and lay people. Create a lay school of theology.

3. Intentional Outreach to the Community

Innovation 1: Plan and carry out an intergenerational service opportunity in October 1996.

Innovation 2: Host a service fair and a monthly emphasis on specific service agencies.

4. Family-Friendly Worship

Innovation 1: Incorporate children and youth into Sunday morning worship in meaningful roles.

Innovation 2: Establish a multigenerational committee to explore various models for family worship by visiting other congregations and researching their program.

Notice how much these innovations vary in type and difficulty. The first innovation under Goal-Oriented Christian Education is a plan that could take many months. Once developed, it would probably not be noticed by many people, yet it represents a necessary first step if the vision being sought by this task force is to be realized.

The first innovation of the second task force, presenting Bibles, is an action that can begin within a few weeks. Once Bibles have arrived for distribution, the accent on Scripture called for in their vision will have begun. Their second innovation, however, is a program that requires far more planning. The task force intends to introduce Bible studies for all levels of interest, offered at varying times and places by both pastoral and lay leaders, and to establish "a lay school of theology." This second innovation will take much time and effort to introduce and sustain, but it is necessary for achieving the vision of this second task force.

The first innovation of the outreach task force is an event that might be developed in fairly short order but one that should give high visibility to the desired outcome of "facilitating a Christian witness and growth in faith through a program of community outreach."

The first innovation of the worship task force involves a policy decision that must be made by those responsible for the worship services. It is a first step toward developing family-friendly worship services. Their second innovation, however, will require more time and effort.

These illustrations show there are many kinds of innovations and that these innovations can vary considerably in how difficult they are to launch. The ideal is that the first innovation can be done quickly and easily to give early visibility to the task force's vision.

A task force is usually involved in not one but several innovations, each of which provides an incremental gain toward achieving the vision. Some members of a task force, however, may remain only long enough to launch the first innovation and will be replaced by others who join the team to be part of its continuing activity.

A task force leader needs to be realistic regarding difficulties likely to be encountered when launching innovations. Hence, each task force must develop a strategy for overcoming resistance and for gaining widespread support relative to its proposed innovation.

The chapters that follow identify the basic steps a task force needs to follow, and reasons why this more time-consuming approach pays off in gaining needed support so the innovations become lasting.

SHIFTING TO TASK FORCES

A pastor who read an earlier manuscript for this book was especially intrigued by this chapter on task forces. His response was, "I like the idea but how does one bring about this kind of revolutionary change in a congregation?"

Establishing task forces is a significant innovation. Ideally they should be introduced using the same steps as those found in our conceptual model. First, establish in people's minds the need for a change, and then present this innovation as an approach that will enhance the mission of the congregation. Tie the innovation to the congregation's mission, and meaningfully involve all whose support is sought for the innovation. Intuitively, Pastor Michael Foss of Prince of Peace Lutheran Church in Burnsville, Minnesota, followed these steps.

First, he reflected with his church council on the need for a change. They agreed committees that had at one time initiated new activities were now gatekeepers and guardians of the status quo. The most exciting ideas were being discussed in the church halls and not in committee meetings. They knew of people who were accustomed to getting something done who refused to be on a committee. The reason they heard was, "I don't have time for this nonsense. I won't sit in a meeting if it is not accomplishing anything."

Aware of the need for a change, the church council decided to separate ministry and governance functions to allow for the spontaneous formation of ministry teams. Therefore, they developed a revision of the constitution that limited the council's responsibilities to oversight, planning and visioning, policy development and adoption, and budget review. Furthermore, they proposed that the ministry of Prince of Peace be organized around ministry teams (task forces) chartered by the church council and empowered to do ministry.

This proposed innovation in governance and ministry was then presented to the congregation for discussion and possible modification at a number of open forums. These meetings, held at different times, provided a chance for members of this 8,000-member congregation to raise questions, gain understanding, and arrive at a sense of ownership.

When I first asked Foss how many ministry teams they now have at Prince of Peace, he said he did not know. Because a ministry team is free to develop spontaneously as needs arise, he had no way of knowing which were currently functioning. He knew of teams that had functioned for six months and some for several years. It all depended on the task and how long certain people wished to be involved.

When I pressed him for an estimate of how many ministry teams were currently in operation, he guessed there were over one thousand ministry teams functioning in the congregation. A study recently completed in his congregation found that a total of 3,500 volunteer hours were being contributed each week to some aspect of ministry. If turned into paid staff activity, these volunteer hours would be the equivalent of eighty-five full-time staff people.

TASK FORCES IN A YOUTH MINISTRY

Youth pastor Richard Ross of Tulip Grove Baptist Church arrived at the idea of task forces out of sheer necessity. His youth program was attracting an increasing number of youth, and his creative mind was seeing new ways to minister to his youth. The problem was that he was becoming an event manager always preparing for the next big thing. He had less time to do what he was trained to do, less time with his family, and less time for his own well-being. Complicating his schedule were his duties as youth minister consultant at the Sunday School Board for the entire Southern Baptist Convention.

A concerned lay youth adviser drew him aside and said he must find another way of carrying out his youth ministry. He was being pulled in too many directions. In response to this counsel, Ross developed a plan to form task forces he calls lead teams. These are teams of youth and adults, ranging in number from ten to fifteen, that assume full responsibility for activities that formerly had been his. These activities include innovative events such as the following:

- An eight-day mission trip to an inner-city area.
- A weekend Disciple Now event, where groups of ten to twelve youth live and fellowship together in one of nine different homes.
- A church camp for seventh and eighth graders at a college campus.

In one year, fifteen events were taken over by fifteen different task forces or lead teams. They met for whatever number of months members felt it was necessary to prepare for their youth event. Key to the success of these teams is the chairperson, one who is chosen with considerable care. When an event is over, the task force disbands.

I listened in on a lead team meeting of six adults and four youth planning for an eight-day mission trip. Its purpose was to involve forty to fifty youth in conducting a vacation Bible school for minority children in an inner city. The chairperson followed a well-developed agenda that included: a detailed budget, a list of lead team assignments, and a grid showing the sequence of classes for each day of vacation Bible school, Monday through Friday.

Most impressive to me was the preparation schedule presented for the team to review. It requested that each Wednesday evening, May 7 to July 9, the forty to fifty youth attend sessions to prepare them for conducting the vacation Bible school. At these sessions they would be given their assignments plus instruction in teaching methods, craft ideas, experience in leading songs, help in presenting object lessons, guidance in how to witness to children, and a general orientation to the trip. Each participant was asked to attend at least seven out of ten meetings and pass a test in order to make the trip.

Here is an example of how a task force activity can equip church members to do the work of ministry in the spirit of Ephesians 4:11-12. Furthermore, it enables youth ministers to shift their time from event and project management to roles in ministry more unique to their calling, training, and gifts.

It is significant that this approach to youth ministry, now being adopted by hundreds of youth ministers, is itself an innovation. Therefore, in his 1997 book *Planning Youth Ministry: From Boot-up to Exit,* Ross gives specific instructions on how to gain a congregation's approval and support for this lead team strategy. His instructions resemble the steps that follow in Part Two of this book, including involving legitimizers and constituencies to gain their counsel and support.

The chapters that follow present the seven steps that make up the FUTURES model, steps a task force should follow to establish lasting innovations. The steps have the added feature of helping members increase their effectiveness as lay ministers.

Reflection:
The Value of Task Forces

• To what extent does maintenance or visionary thinking characterize our present committees?

• Are the committees we now have able to focus on an activity of special interest, or must they be concerned about a broad area of responsibility?

• What characterizes the team most likely to stay focused on launching a needed ministry and persevering until it is well established?

• How difficult would it be to shift from standing committees to task forces?

PART TWO

THE FUTURES MODEL

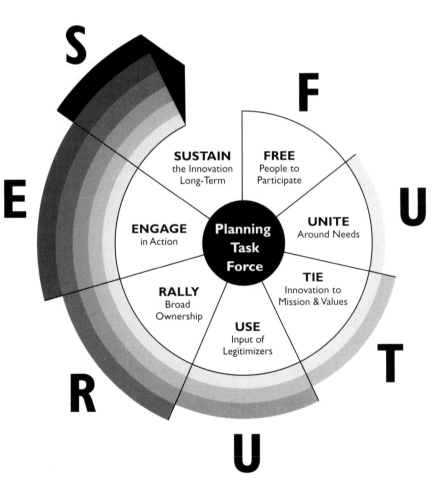

CHAPTER FOUR

FREE PEOPLE
TO PARTICIPATE IN
EFFECTING CHANGE

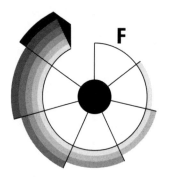

"Good leaders are evaluated in terms of their ability to create enthusiasm. They must believe in the impossible."

—*Tom Peters and Robert Waterman*

THE FIRST ESSENTIAL in fostering a congregation's readiness to respond is an atmosphere that frees people to participate in effecting needed change. Such an atmosphere is engendered by a culture that seeks to develop the gifts of members and equip them for ministry to others.

Though this chapter primarily addresses the pastor, the qualities identified as important for a pastor are qualities also needed by lay leaders in a congregation. The style of leadership advocated here is important for all who serve on a task force or church council and for all who serve as teachers, youth leaders, or lay visitors.

The first consideration in our FUTURES model relates to leadership style. Here the Innovation Study provides clear direction. First, it shows how important atmosphere is with respect to a group's readiness to act. And, second, it shows how dependent this atmosphere is on a leader's style of leadership—how he or she relates to people. Members sense whether or not their pastors are:

- committed to enhancing the effectiveness of their congregation
  - supportive and affirming of members
  - open to and encouraging of new ideas

A pastor's attitude, words, and actions establish an atmosphere in a congregation that is conducive to or resistant to effecting needed change. The relationship you establish with your members is all-important. When your comments reflect a personal commitment to improvement, or people sense that you support innovative ideas and encourage creativity, you will see the emergence of an open and progressive atmosphere. It means, however, in the words of Richard Hutcheson, you need to be "comfortable in an open system, with mystery, with surprise, and with God's intervention."[1]

It should be noted that people in a congregation, even the infrequent visitor, perceive quite accurately the pastor's style of leadership and the atmosphere of the congregation. When the pastor is not open, affirming, and supportive, this is quickly sensed. The perceptions of members are worth taking seriously.[2]

Freeing people to participate, the first step in our conceptual model, is important because it encourages high morale, group enthusiasm, creative solutions to emerging problems, and a positive attitude toward change. In the Innovation Study, we found that congregations reflecting such an atmosphere typically attracted large numbers to their meetings, found creative solutions to emerging problems, and reflected higher morale and group enthusiasm.

By way of contrast, a controlling atmosphere showed up as fostering division, acquiescence, apathy, and a dullness that shackled the desire and readiness of these congregations to act.

When a pastor's style of leadership includes a commitment to needed change, an affirming attitude toward members, and an openness to experimentation and new ideas, the atmosphere is warmed and becomes freeing. In such churches, members tend to enjoy their work and feel as though they are part of a team. They are proud of how their group functions and enthusiastic about what their congregation accomplishes. A leader's style of approach to the people being served, shapes the atmosphere and culture of a congregation.

Cultures can be characterized by one of four words: control, collaboration, competence, or cultivation. These classifications were developed by William Schneider, an organizational consultant, based on his work with business organizations. His classifications were originally formed to describe what he saw in secular institutions, but they also describe cultures found in congregations.

Although no congregation is purely one culture or another, the distinctions are useful because they square with what is commonly observed.

CULTURE AND LEADERSHIP STYLES

Control Culture

According to Schneider, the motivation underlying a control culture is the need of its leaders for power, enhanced by a fear of being vulnerable. Order, predictability, and the maintenance of stability are deemed important. A control culture prizes objectivity and externally generated facts. It shies away from emotions, subjectivity and "soft" ideas. The leadership style tends to be highly methodical, careful and conservative.[3]

I became conscious of this control culture when making my first visit to a congregation in October 1958 to collect survey information. It was one of the randomly selected congregations in our national study of Lutheran youth. Here is what I wrote in my diary:

> The church council impressed me by their lack of concern and their feeling of satisfaction with the status quo. The pastor for the past 17 years was feared and obeyed. A strong sense of duty prevails in the church and a willing obedience. The early church constitution began, "Since the law of God demands . . . [And later,] any officer who fails to . . . shall lose his membership."

> Membership is important here. Ladies honor anniversaries (25th) if the person has been a member of the Aid for at least five years. Those who sign the "black book" become voting

members. There are about 110 such members and these are given special consideration in contrast to non-members.

The stewardship approach is governed by what is needed to maintain the present program. Benevolences are paid out of the yearly surplus. New members are cautioned to not pledge too high—"we don't need it."

The new pastor (with whom I spoke) kept wondering, while admiring the traditions of strong loyalty and respect, whether the motivation is duty or spiritual life. There has been a traditional reserve between pastor and people. As a result he, as new pastor, has found little opportunity to know what his people think.

This control culture may have been more common in the past, but it is still found. Reference is made to it in the 1995 report of a national study of a denomination, *Congregations at Crossroads*. It identifies a pattern in the church: active leaders and passive parishioners. The report speaks of having found "a culture that encourages strong leaders who 'have all the answers' and encourages parishioners to rely too heavily on their pastors for leadership, guidance, and strategies."[4]

Every denomination has pastors who wish to control everything that happens in their parish. They stress organization and procedure as well as the cognitive side of faith and usually emphasize the need for correct doctrines. Their ministry tends to be legalistic and lacking in personal warmth.

Collaborative Culture

This culture, according to Schneider, uses the family as its prototype. It is motivated by a strong need to have friends and close relationships with other people. Partnerships, interaction, and teamwork are strongly encouraged. In this culture members feel a commitment to the organization, and the organization feels a commitment to its people.[5]

Lyle Schaller, a church consultant who has visited thousands of congregations in dozens of denominations, insists that size of congregation is a most important variable because it affects the quality of congregational life. Small churches, he observes, tend to resemble families and thus emphasize fellowship, relationships, intimacy, belonging, and involvement. People matter more than performance. The small church expects the minister to love the members. Relationship-building is deemed more important than excellent preaching or other aspects of ministry.

But the weakness of this culture is its tendency to center on one's church family and to lack a mission outreach. According to Schaller, once people have as many ties as they want or can handle, they may remain congenial to newcomers but will offer them only superficial friendliness. Such churches become "closed."[6]

The weakness of this culture is also identified in the *Church Membership Initiative*, a study of Lutheran churches completed in 1993. It reports that though a majority of Lutherans say they want growth, most "consistently and overtly oppose doing what is necessary to foster growth." This is evident in their unwillingness to modify such things as worship style, liturgy, program content, style of ministry, or whatever needs changing in order to reach others. Congregations of this culture are not open to change.[7]

Competence Culture

The university provides the prototype for what Schneider calls a competence culture—one that strongly emphasizes expertise and the advancement of knowledge. Most organizations that reflect this culture tend to be research centers and agencies that develop patents, creative theories, scientific discoveries, and new technologies and services. In this culture one who wishes to be accorded esteem must demonstrate competence. Success is tied to being the best.[8]

Schaller observes that large congregations tend to focus on competence. They are qualitatively different from small congregations in that members are apt to look for performance more than relationships. They want quality programs, well-organized activities and professional leadership. Therefore, the senior minister should be highly skilled in administration, supervision, and leadership of both large and small groups.[9]

There are pastors whose ministry reflects a high level of competence. They attract people of competence to their congregation and encourage their members to excel by challenging them with possibilities. Some of these pastors gain national visibility through their television, radio, and publication ministries. Their congregations could be characterized as competence cultures because members are conscious of being pacesetters in various aspects of ministry.

The danger within this culture is becoming status-conscious, dependent on recognition, and unwilling to accept anything but favorable feedback. For congregations with this culture, success becomes subtly identified with a large membership, outstanding programs, and ample finances.

Cultivation Culture

A church with a cultivation culture wishes to see change, development, and growth in the people it serves. It is a culture dedicated to furthering the human spirit, to inculcating ethics and values, and to establishing a system of beliefs and expectations. Its style of leadership gives people considerable personal freedom and autonomy and encourages self-expression and the cultivation of talents and abilities.[10]

Pastors with this style of leadership are motivated by a strong desire to involve people in a life of faith. The resulting culture is found in growing congregations. *The Church Membership Initiative* says of such churches:

> Clergy in growing congregations function with a shared vision of the congregation within the community. They have a clear sense of themselves and a sense of shared trust with the laity. They function with a sense of the "priesthood of all believers" by surfacing gifts possessed by members and empowering those members to use their gifts. They are not controlling. These clergy view ministry as a partnership, not as "my" ministry.[11]

Such pastors cultivate lay leaders in the congregation, who in turn carry out the congregation's ministry. The pastors are less involved in maintenance activities and more involved in initiating new programs that challenge members to grow in faith and service.

This is the culture that characterizes Iglesia Evangelica Unida de Puerto Rico, a congregation of 260 members found to be exemplary in the Effective Christian Education Study. This national study of Protestant congregations, reported in 1990, was conducted by Search Institute. Its purpose was to assess the extent to which expressions of faith and loyalty characterize adolescents, Christian educators, pastors, and other adults of six major denominations. The denominations included the Christian Church (Disciples of Christ), Evangelical Lutheran Church in America, Presbyterian Church (U.S.A.), United Church of Christ, United Methodist Church, and Southern Baptist Convention. Over eleven thousand people randomly drawn from 561 congregations participated in completing paper-and-pencil surveys. A unique feature of the study was identifying congregations that scored high on measures of faith and loyalty, and visiting those congregations to identify factors contributing to their high scores.

The researcher who visited Iglesia Evangelica Unida de Puerto Rico wrote:

> Everybody feels part of the church, including the children and everybody has the opportunity to use their gifts to contribute to the life of the church. . . . After our interviews with the various teachers, groups and persons, we concluded that in this church the people mature in faith by practicing it. They practice it from the time they are children. People are not afraid to talk the language of faith and to express themselves using theological concepts and language.

In this congregation where 60 percent of its members have a college degree, prayer and the study of Scripture have become important ways for members to participate in the life of the congregation. Every Tuesday night people gather for a prayer service, which for some begins with fasting the night before. Approximately 150 to 175 are present for prayer and the sharing of testimonies. The next evening they gather for Bible study, where the intent is to discover the will of God for the present moment and to address issues relating to their life as Christians. The result is a cultivation culture.

Evaluating the Four Cultures

Two cultures: collaboration and cultivation, are personal and result from a style of leadership that encourages a freeing atmosphere. A collaboration culture, however, tends to shy away from innovation because its members are likely to resist changes designed to reach people outside their family circle. By contrast, the cultivation culture's leaders are primarily focused on mission and are deeply concerned that members be actively involved in sharing and service.

Though a competence culture fosters a competitive atmosphere, it does emphasize possibilities. Though a control culture fosters a passive membership, it does promote order, predictability, and stability. The culture to strive for, however, is a cultivation culture—which this book discusses more fully in subsequent chapters. Innovative ways are encouraged in order to carry out a more effective ministry.

CHANGING A CULTURE

A culture change may be necessary before a congregation can be ready to act. Such a change may require a deliberate change in the pastor's style of leadership. This is sometimes necessary. Top leaders of Seattle's Boeing Company became overwhelmingly convinced that a change in style of leadership was what they needed. They came to see that bringing about a cultural change was the only way they could remain competitive as a world-class organization.

One Boeing manager, Gordon Tagge, described what his company did to change the leadership style of their managers.

Awareness of a Need for Change

At the Boeing Company in Seattle, Chairman Frank Schrontz became aware of how the competition and business environment were changing. By 1988, most Fortune 500 companies listed twenty years earlier had either made significant changes in their company or were being viewed as unhealthy; many had already gone out of business.

Most of Boeing's work in Seattle is done by the Boeing Commercial Company. Its president, Dean Thornton, asked Bruce Gising to develop a plan for world-class competitiveness. One of the initial steps in this plan was to visit a number of successful worldwide industries. A consulting firm was hired to help identify what to look for and what questions to ask.

After visiting a number of successful industries, Gising returned with the observation, "We don't know how bad a company we have." He strongly recommended that Thornton make a similar visit to see firsthand what is happening elsewhere. Thornton and other officials visited selected Japanese industries and reported their observations. When Thornton, addressed his executives, he stated, "You don't know how bad we are."

Commitment to an Innovative Style of Management

As a result of this awareness, the Boeing company made an investment of over $300 million to effect a massive cultural change identified as Continuous Quality Improvement. This required a revolutionary shift in the way management did its work. Two top officials in the company, Frank Schrontz and Phil Condit, told managers that "old ways of success that focused on results, and not on how we get them, are no longer to be perpetuated."

That cryptic sentence called attention to a revolutionary shift in how management was to be carried out. Hundreds of managers and supervisors needed to learn and understand the principles underlying core competencies that are at the heart of making a company great. Lest a commitment to this change in management style be slow in coming, a letter from Schrontz and Condit informed them that "Boeing would evaluate, promote, and retain managers on the basis of attributes which include: 'Leads Continuous Quality Improvement focused on customer satisfaction'; 'Treats people with fairness, trust and respect'; 'Removes barriers, promotes teamwork, and empowers people to improve business performance'; 'Shares information, listens to others, and maintains objectivity'; and 'Coaches people to develop their capabilities.'" These attributes resemble those identified through the Innovation Study, ones that make for a freeing and creative atmosphere.

Boeing then determined that this cultural change would be best achieved by using people within the organization who are respected and experienced members of the company. Within each division, qualified individuals were chosen to serve as "Master Coaches," to conduct a two-year program of teaching to establish a servant/leader attitude among the managers. The intent was to establish a threat-free environment characterized by open avenues of communication. It was to alter the basic stance of employees, who in effect have been saying, "You can buy my back and my performance but you can't buy my heart, mind, incentive, or ability to show you how this job can be done better." The intent also was to involve employees in evaluating ideas to improve how things are done and in reshaping them before sending them back to management.

Outcomes of the Cultural Shift

When the new 777 Boeing airplane was completed, its unveiling became the occasion for celebrating the product of a total team effort. It symbolized what could be accomplished when there is a focus on the relationship between workers, management, and customer. It marked a change in the climate and atmosphere of an entire company, a change that occurred when its leadership adopted a style of management that focused on the customer (recipient of the services), fostered a sense of partnership, and encouraged broad ownership of what was being done.

This illustration underscores the importance of how a leader relates to the people served. The culture that is established is one that facilitates or hinders the ability of an organization to carry out its mission.

CHARACTERISTICS OF INNOVATIVE LEADERSHIP

What creates a freeing atmosphere and establishes a cultivation culture in a congregation? Two things are important: a sense of mission and a freeing approach to people. The latter quality is reflected in these two quotes. "Good leaders are evaluated in terms of their ability to create enthusiasm. They must be people who believe in the impossible," and "Leaders . . . are evangelists for the dream."[12]

It would be hard to overstate the importance of this ability of a leader to create enthusiasm. It is both a learned and spontaneous quality of optimism and hope that for members of a congregation is infectious. The leader expects God is going to bless future events and provide growth and development in exciting ways. The leader also sees failure as a matter due to a procedure or situation that can be changed, thus enabling one to succeed next time around.

Martin Seligman, a psychologist at the University of Pennsylvania, studied insurance salesmen at MetLife. He found that new salespeople who were by nature optimists sold 37 percent more insurance in their first two years than did pessimists. During the first year the pessimists quit at twice the rate of the optimists.[13] The evidence is strong that organizational innovativeness is associated with a warm, open, and enthusiastic atmosphere, of which one of the best indications is high staff and member morale.[14]

Our Innovation Study identified three characteristics of leaders that help create an innovative, and freeing atmosphere.

Commitment to Change

First, the leader is visibly committed to making whatever changes will improve the congregation's ministry.

This commitment to change flows out of a pastor's deep desire to see Christ's kingdom advanced. The pastor is willing to make whatever changes will enhance the effectiveness of the congregation without compromising the mission or message of Jesus Christ, and is willing to be contemporary without compromising. Such a stance involves being open to criticism, suggestions, and new ideas. It means being willing to listen to others, consider possibilities, and seek solutions.

A fundamental shift of mind should not be alien to a pastor or religious leader whose tradition centers in the Greek word *metanoia.* This word, which has a rich history, describes a fundamental change or shift in one's thinking. For Christians, who have been directed by John the Baptist and Jesus Christ to repent (turn and go in another direction), the idea of such a change is familiar. It is what the Christian church is in the business to effect.

Not every pastor or lay leader, however, is willing to introduce needed change. And this commitment or lack of it is evident to members of a congregation. Examples of members' perceptions are found in the items forming the cluster called Commitment to Change (see sidebar 4.1.)

This cluster is formed because there are people who see their leaders as committed to making needed changes and people who do not see this characteristic in their leaders. Both groups hold this construct unconsciously in their minds when responding to the items. Because their responses are subtly influenced by the construct, the items intercorrelate.

A commitment to change does not necessarily call for drastic change. Change can involve small improvements. That for instance, is what characterizes Japan's approach to leadership. Their postwar "economic miracle" has been premised on a style of leadership called KAIZEN, a word that means "improvement." This philosophy seeks improvement in everything and everyone— people's working life, social life, and home life. It involves going beyond maintenance to improving the present situation, and at times might include significant innovations. It is a true cultivation culture.

When leaders are committed to change, the groups they serve are more innovative in carrying out their work. When we returned after three years to organizations in the Innovation Study, we found that groups whose members saw their leaders as committed to change were far more involved in such innovative activities as evaluating their staff and program, introducing new programs, making use of outside specialists in areas of concern, conducting training sessions for volunteer leaders, trying new methods or procedures, and seeking creative solutions to emerging problems.[15]

Open and Affirming

Second, the leader treats people in an affirming, trusting, and supportive way. The supporting evidence for this characteristic is quite overwhelming. It comes from a million-dollar study of pastors in forty-seven denominations carried out by Search Institute in 1983 for the Association of Theological Schools in the United States and Canada. One purpose of the study was to determine the criteria lay people use when evaluating the effectiveness of their pastor.[16]

The dimension of ministry that drew the highest rating, open and affirming style,. includes the following elements:

1. Remains positive and affirming of people even when handling stressful situations.

2. Is willing to acknowledge own limitations and personal mistakes.

3. Shows a flexibility of spirit in being willing to hear differing views and welcome new possibilities.

4. Honors commitments and carries out personal promises.

This list carries some resemblance to the characteristics of overseers compiled by the writer of 1 Timothy: "above reproach, . . . temperate, self-controlled, respectable, hospitable, . . . gentle, not quarrelsome, not a lover of money, . . . have a good reputation with others" (3:2-7). Though the two lists are not identical, they describe in similar fashion the style of leadership people covet in their pastor.[17]

Note how these descriptions from Timothy square with the definitions of social intelligence given by Daniel Goleman in his groundbreaking book, *Emotional Intelligence: Why it Can Matter More Than IQ*:

> Men who are high in emotional intelligence are socially poised, outgoing and cheerful, not prone to fearfulness. They have a notable capacity for commitment to people or causes, for taking responsibility, and for having an ethical outlook; they are sympathetic and caring in their relationships.[18]

Significantly, the world of business is finding that the virtuoso in interpersonal skills is important in the corporate future—that leadership is not domination but the art of persuading people to work for a common goal.[19] The cost-effectiveness of social intelligence is why Seattle Boeing spent millions to shift managers' style of leadership to one that involves social intelligence.

Note the items in sidebar 4.2 from the Innovation Study, which describe the kind of support members especially appreciate.

When members feel affirmed by their leader, they are far more likely to volunteer for tasks and participate in them with warmth and enthusiasm. The effect, though subtle, is real. When we returned to congregations in the Innovation Study whose pastors were perceived by members and staff as being warm and supportive, we found these effects: larger numbers of volunteer leaders, a greater concern for people among the youth, a larger number of youth in the youth group, and systematic planning.

A friend sent me an excellent summary of the research on service professionals, such as nurses, doctors, teachers, counselors, and social workers. The studies showed that the best predictors of success in a service profession were not grades, knowledge, or competence. Rather, they were found in the attitude and spirit of the professionals, namely, how they viewed people, task, and self. Similarly, in a separate study of medical doctors, we found that the best predictors of success were concern for people and moral integrity, not skill or competence.

Our data underscore the importance of leaders verbalizing appreciation of the people with whom they work and supporting creative efforts in visible ways. Recognizing an individual's contributions to the success of a project can create self-fulfilling prophecies. When encouraged by appreciation, ordinary people can achieve extraordinary results. The modeling they see in a pastor increases the likelihood they will show a caring attitude, a concern for people, and a deepening prayer life.

Being an affirming and supportive person is an important aspect of leadership. It fosters a culture that is personal and serves as a stimulus for growth. It encourages people to risk failure, because they realize that if they fail, they can learn from the experience.

Encourages Creativity

Third, the leader fosters the freedom, and flexibility of spirit needed for innovative thinking.

Peter Senge, in *The Fifth Discipline*, identifies this type of leadership as the kind that fosters a climate "where it is safe for people to create visions, where inquiry and commitment to the truth are the norm, and where challenging the status quo is expected—especially when the status quo is obscuring aspects of reality that people seek to avoid."[20]

C. Argyris, a pioneer in organizational studies, makes an interesting observation. People have been "programmed" in the past for a behavioral style that is based on being controlled and on avoiding negative criticism. (Note how this is true also for congregations. Members may withhold negative comments until they are out in the parking lot where people can feel free to express how they really feel.) For some, therefore, it is an adjustment to take the initiative in congregational matters and express opinions and give suggestions.[21]

Nothing undermines openness more surely than a leader who is always certain. Once a group is given an answer with finality and a "don't contradict me" stance, all motivation to question what has been said disappears. Unspoken thoughts are driven underground. What is lost are the ideas, intuitive insights, and hunches that come to people through the leading of God's Spirit. Intuitive responses often result in creative solutions—breakthroughs that are not the result of rational, linear thinking.[22]

Members sense when the pastor's style of leadership conveys freedom to disagree or offer other ideas. People see this openness as more than a set of pastoral skills and practices. It is experienced as a spirit, a quality of relationships, that can be identified as an expression of love. Openness defined in this way has to do with intentions—the commitment to serve one another, the willingness to be vulnerable in that service.[23]

Some aspects of openness that respondents in the Innovation Study notice with appreciation, characteristics of leadership that make for an innovative atmosphere, are noted in sidebar 4.3. Note what is included in the items that form this cluster: freedom to experiment, to take independent action, to innovate, and flexibility in administrative procedures. Groups in the Innovation Study that ranked their unit high on this dimension were found, after three years, to have broken with traditional ways of doing things and to have made significant improvements.[24]

Peter Senge points out that a leader can achieve control without controlling by moving decisions down the organizational hierarchy in what he calls "localness"—extending authority and power as far from the top as possible. This means unleashing people's commitment by giving them freedom to act, to try out their ideas and be responsible for achieving results.[25]

Pastor Jerry Hoffman of Nativity Lutheran Church in Minneapolis, Minnesota, has taken this leadership approach by introducing an organizational structure that provides the opportunity for people who see a need to respond in the form of a task force. He dispensed with standing committees except for two governance groups that provide direction and overall supervision of whatever task forces are spontaneously formed to address emerging needs. These governance groups review proposals of task forces and authorize anticipated expenditures to achieve the objectives identified in the proposal.

A pastor or leader who is cultivating a control culture will not feel comfortable encouraging creativity. He or she will fear that things will get out of hand, that ambitious people will take over, that wrong doctrine will be taught, or that some people might be offended by proposed changes. But such an approach to leadership hardly serves the kingdom of Jesus Christ.

Some pastors are seen as resisting changes members feel are needed in their congregation. Their theological or biblical rationale for an opposing position is often perceived as a thinly disguised desire to be seen as the ultimate authority. A control pastor's negative effect on parishioners is illustrated in studies of capable business managers whose leadership was viewed as flawed.

V. J. Benz, a research psychologist, published the first study of this problem under the heading "managerial derailment." His focus was on root causes for senior executives being promoted, or dismissed, at Sears in the 1950s and 1960s. Though all executives were bright, assertive, self-confident, and self-disciplined, some nonetheless failed. The qualities associated with their failure included being overcontrolling, arrogant, and playing politics. One of these qualities alone was sufficient to serve as the overriding flaw in preventing an executive from building a team.

Similarly, research at the Center for Creative Leadership, Greensboro, North Carolina, led to the conclusion that managers who derail are perceived by associates as indecisive, micromanaging, abrasive, too ambitious, or aloof. These qualities erode their ability to recruit and motivate a team. Supportive of this conclusion are other studies on organizational climate over a period of four decades. These studies show that 60 to 75 percent of employees typically report that the worst aspect of their job is their immediate supervisor. For these employees, the controlling ways of their supervisor is a constant irritant.[26]

By way of contrast, the encouragement of creativity by congregational leaders, though it may have its risks, motivates, energizes, and otherwise inspires members of a team, group, or congregation. It is a characteristic associated with competent management and inspired leadership.

Reflection:
My Congregation's Climate

What is the dominant culture in my congregation? Is it:

- Well organized, with decisions coming from the top down?
- Friendly and cozy, with very little outreach to strangers?
- Well endowed with people who delight in things being done well?
- Rich in opportunities for everybody to develop and use their gifts in ministry?

What characterizes my leadership style?

- Am I visibly committed to making whatever changes will improve the congregation's ministry?
- Do I treat people in an affirming, trusting, and supportive way?
- Do I foster the freedom and flexibility of spirit needed for innovative thinking?

Because a pastor's style of leadership establishes over time the culture of a congregation, a necessary first step in bringing about needed change is to free people to participate as lay ministers. Once freed and encouraged to assume responsibility for emerging needs, laity become a significant force for good. They become aware of the concerns of people around them, concerns discussed in the next chapter.

CHAPTER FIVE

UNITE AROUND NEEDS

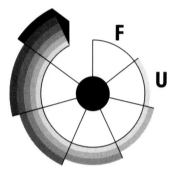

People change when they:
- *Hurt enough that they have to change;*
- *Learn enough that they want to change;*
- *Receive enough that they are able to change.*

—*John Maxwell*

TO INTRODUCE A CHANGE OR INNOVATION for which a group has no felt need is to court failure. An awareness of need and a felt pressure to act are both necessary. For a need to become a driving force, it must be felt by all whose involvement is needed.

Consider the following two illustrations of congregations that in responding to needs around them have become growing congregations.

THE STORY OF LONE WOLF

When Pastor William Geis came to St. John's Lutheran Church at Lone Wolf, Oklahoma, he found a dying congregation in a dying community. In a county with no more than ten people per square mile, it was no longer possible to maintain a viable commercial center. Most stores had moved out and many houses were vacant and boarded up. Buildings that were still occupied could only give hints of a glory long past.

St. John's, a struggling church, had cut back its program to worship services, funerals, and weddings. Little was being done for the children and youth. The other churches in the community did little more. The effects of their gross neglect were apparent in the teenage pregnancies, alcoholism, and drug use that plagued the school's student body.

Pastor Geis determined that St. John's would not continue with business as usual. Rather it would help the community develop. It would become an island of hope. St. John's would become a growing congregation in spite of the declining demographics. He began by involving his small membership in identifying concerns about the community (for example, the future of the schools, neglected kids, lack of stores, no jobs). Together they envisioned what they could do (for example, make the church facilities available, sponsor activities for the community, cooperate with other churches). Motivated by a vision of what they could do, the congregation has entered into the life of the community and restored hope. Its members have taken responsibility for adding to the ministries of the congregation. (For example, in a given week there are fourteen Bible studies.) The enthusiasm of members has attracted outsiders to make this congregation a growing one.[1]

THE STORY OF TRI-COUNTY MINISTRY

Seven Lutheran churches and one Presbyterian Church in a three-county area around Binford, North Dakota, found themselves facing the same need. All were without a pastor. All had serious financial limitations.

Faced with this pressing need that threatened the existence of their congregations, their leaders were willing to consider an idea floated by a staff member from the synod office. The idea was to form Tri-County Parish, a proposal that had its strong detractors. By doing so, however, they were able to call a lead pastor, a youth and education pastor, a visitation pastor, and an intern. Assisting them is a parish coordinator and two secretaries. Each person serves the entire parish.

As a result of cooperating in this way, the eight congregations have stability. (If one pastor resigns, there are still three left to maintain the ministry.) The multiple staff eliminates the feeling of isolation that plagues so many rural pastors. Each pastor can work in the area where he or she is most gifted.

Most importantly, the small congregations are strengthened and given a greater vision when joined with other churches. A member of one church said, "Before Tri–County started we had between eight and fifteen in worship and now we have between thirty-five and fifty. There is a renewed spirit."

Specialization has been especially helpful as far as the youth ministry in this parish is concerned. "Before Tri-County we had very little happening with our youth because we had so few. Now the youth have someone who focuses specifically on them with a number of events to choose from." The council president, Roger Miller, evaluated the success of this pioneering effort: "We think this model is a key part of the future of rural ministry."[2] The success of this innovation caught the news media's attention, and a write-up appeared in the *New York Times*.[3]

NO MORE "BUSINESS AS USUAL"

One need that cannot be ignored is one that faces congregations of all mainline congregations. It has to do with trends in church giving and church membership. If unchecked, these trends could signal the end of denominations.

In *Behind the Stained Glass Windows: Money Dynamics in the Church*, John and Sylvia Ronsvalle provide the evidence.[4] Using data from the past twenty-six years for eleven mainline denominations, they were able to establish a clear trend in church giving from 1968 to 1993. When this trend line is projected into the future, the result (assuming no change occurs) is the end to denominational support by the year A.D. 2032.

The same story can be told with respect to congregational finances. When data from twenty-nine denominations from 1968 to 1993 are combined, the trend is that (assuming again that no change occurs) giving will have ceased by A.D. 2032.

Equally sobering is the trend showing a decline in church membership. Denominations that have grown without interruption from colonial days now see declines. According to the Ronsvalles, church membership as a percentage of our countries population, if unchecked, will fall to 0 percent of the U.S. population in less than one hundred years.

This evidence cries out for a willingness to break old patterns and press for a more vital, mission-oriented approach to ministry.

Clearly, a profound shift in societal values and people's view of the church has occurred in the past few decades, creating for Christians a new awareness of needs. The shift has changed the context within which a congregation serves, and it has changed people's concept of mission. The mission field is no longer found only in foreign lands but out the front door of the church.

Loren Mead, founder and past president of the Alban Institute, who has spent forty or more of his years working in, with, and for Christian congregations, has distilled his experience in *The Once and Future Church*. He identifies two paradigms that have formed the context and mission of the church. The first was the Apostolic Paradigm in which the local incarnation of the church was a tight community of convinced, committed, and embattled believers supporting each other within a hostile environment.

With the conversion of Emperor Constantine in A.D. 313 came the Christendom Paradigm. The congregation became a parish, and those born in that area automatically became members of the church. This paradigm, continued over the centuries, finds clearest expression in the state churches of Europe.

Though not maintained officially, this paradigm has been the operative model in the United States. Clergy have assumed a strong, central, and unquestioned role—a high-status role that carries authority. Congregations, part of the social glue of this nation, have grounded their institutions in the biblical story and given words and ideas to America's great moments. The church has determined many of the laws of the land. Mead contends that this paradigm is falling apart and that a new one needs to be formed.[5]

One reason for the old paradigm's falling apart is the shift that has occurred in dominant worldviews. That is the opinion of Armand Nicholi Jr., associate clinical professor of psychiatry at the Harvard Medical School. He believes that "no two men have made a more indelible impact on the world we live in today that Karl Marx and Sigmund Freud. They have helped change our particular society from one whose values were primarily moral and spiritual to one whose values are primarily material and secular."[6]

An illustration of this shift is found in the changes that have occurred in the governing philosophy of Harvard University, a school that serves as a prototype for what is happening in the universities and colleges of the country. Here is the account by Kelly Monroe from her book *Finding God at Harvard.*

Harvard was founded in 1636 that students might be free to know the truth and life in relation to Jesus Christ. Thus, the early mottoes were *Veritas* ("Truth," 1643), *In Christi Gloriam* ("To the Glory of Christ"), and *Christo et Ecclesiae* ("For Christ and the Church," 1692).

The display of three open books on the early seal, two facing up and one facing down, suggested the dynamic relationship between reason and revelation. One of the earliest accounts of Harvard, the College Laws of 1642, reads:

> Let every student . . . consider the main end of his life and studies is to know God and Jesus Christ which is eternal life, John 17:3, and therefore to lay Christ in the bottom, as the only foundation of all sound knowledge and learning. Seeing the Lord giveth wisdom, everyone shall seriously by prayer, in secret, seek wisdom of Him.

Today the popular *Veritas* shield no longer includes Christ and the church. It is no news that classical Christian thought is politically, socially, and even theologically incorrect at Harvard. Believers are often considered members of a counterculture. Some students feel marginalized in the classroom, not because they are African-American, Asian-American, or international students but primarily because they are Christian believers.[7]

George G. Hunter, whose goal for twenty-five years or more has been to reach the secular person, makes this observation in *How to Reach Secular People:* "The secularization process by which the church lost the central place and influence it enjoyed in the centuries of 'Christendom,' has produced a vast mission field in the western world. In today's secular West, the church no longer enjoys a 'home court advantage.' The church now faces the challenge of reevangelizing Europe and North America."[8]

We see evidence of secularization in the removal of religious symbols from the public sector, in the paucity of references to religion in school textbooks, in the commercialization of Sunday, and in school policies that make religion appear irrelevant or even harmful.

Secularization is very apparent in the realm of scholarship. Less than 2 percent of the hundreds of thousands of research studies carried out by psychologists include the religious variable,[9] even though it can be demonstrated empirically that religious beliefs and values are the best predictors of what people say and do.

Secularization has also made its impact on the home and church. Today people in most homes rarely discuss God, the Bible, or matters of faith. This fact became dramatically evident when we asked over eight thousand young adolescents (grades 5–9) whose parents were members of a Protestant or Roman Catholic church how often they as a family discussed God or the Bible or some religious issues. Though 97 percent of the parents belong to a major Christian denomination, 44 percent of their adolescents said such discussions never happened; 32 percent said they may happen once a month; and 13 percent said "once a week," leaving around 10 percent for whom this ancient tradition is maintained with any degree of regularity.[10]

With a secularized society has come a moral vacuum. Striking evidence of this is found in the statistics given in a speech by the former secretary of education, William Bennett. Based on "The Index of Leading Cultural Indicators" released through the auspices of the Heritage Foundation, Bennett says in his essay, "Redeeming Our Time":

> Between the years 1960–1990, there was a 560 percent increase in violent crime; more than a 400 percent increase in illegitimate births; a quadrupling in divorce; a tripling of the percentage of children living in single-parent homes; more than a 200 percent increase in the suicide rate; and a drop of 75 points in the average SAT scores of high school students. Today, 30 percent of all births and 68 percent of black births are illegitimate. The top problems for teachers in our schools are: drug use, alcohol abuse, pregnancy, suicide, rape, robbery, and assault.[11]

It is obvious that lives need changing—and this is precisely the business of the church. The message of the Christian faith is to repent. to turn around, to change *(metanoia).* And to communicate that message more effectively to people who are going in the wrong direction, changes need to be made in how congregations reach out to the secular person and those who are troubled, struggling, or lost.

But changes do not sell themselves. Groups must be helped to bring about changes they view as necessary. Societal trends that are impacting congregations make it imperative that its leaders rethink traditional ways of doing ministry. Changes are needed in the how (not the what) of a congregation's ministry.

BECOMING AWARE OF COMMUNITY NEEDS

Leaders of Central Christian church of Decatur, Illinois, have become aware of needs in their community. Although some years ago, a storm severely damaged this church, whose worship attendance was down to ninety-three, this church within seventeen years has become a large congregation. It was singled out for special visits by a research team because the youth and adults of this congregation scored exceptionally high on a careful measure of faith indicators. They had participated with 561 randomly selected Protestant congregations in the national Effective Christian Education Study.[13]

To rebuild their church, this congregation organized its program of Christian education around families. It has come to be known as a "warm, caring, family-like community of Christians." Members see faith as something to live out. Hence, there is a churchwide emphasis on acting on one's faith and serving those in the community.

DOVE (Disciples of Voluntary Effort) is a service agency founded by this congregation but now supported by thirty-four Protestant and Roman Catholic churches in their area. It provides a wide range of programs and services expanded to cover a five-county area. It offers a residential shelter for victims of domestic violence, including a crisis hotline, legal assistance, services for parents and children, and a treatment center for male abusers. It trains and places over 350 volunteers who are over sixty years of age in more than fifty community agencies. A mother-to-mother program for friendship and support links suburban white women with welfare mothers, most of whom are of color. DOVE also provides preschool opportunities, a clothing room, and a community organization for low income residents. Most of the staff and many of the volunteer leaders are members of Central Christian Church.

When federal funding for the VISTA program was cut, the congregation organized SARF (Service Agency Rescue Fund) and raised enough funds to continue the salaries of two VISTA workers. It started the first nursery school in the city available to the entire community. It is actively committed to a program of study, prayer, and work for global peace and justice. It is the largest contributor to the denomination's mission fund.[13]

Adopting a Listening Stance

A congregation's ministry must reflect an awareness of the profound changes occurring in our communities. Hence, a first priority is to take a sober look at compelling needs a church can address. This requires a listening stance, a deliberate effort to become aware of the visible and hidden needs of members and community. Rick Warren, in *The Purpose Driven Church*, tells of how this listening stance helped him determine how he would establish his ministry in Saddleback Valley, California. He came to know the interests, concerns, and attitudes toward church, that characterized those he hoped to reach for Christ.[14]

In our study of Catholic schools, we found a high correlation between systematically listening to what people feel is needed and the introduction of new and better ways of teaching. We also found that schools and congregations that systematically listen to what constituencies have to say do a better job of sustaining worthwhile changes. They tend to introduce fewer but longer lasting innovations.

The evidence is clear: the more conscious a group is of the needs it might meet, the greater is the likelihood of its effecting changes to meet that need. The gap between vision and current reality can become a source of creative energy. If there is no perception of a gap, people will feel no need for any action to move toward the vision. But if a gap is seen and a concern is generated that this gap be bridged, the leader has established a creative tension that motivates people both to act and to accept needed change.[15]

Pastor John Maxwell of the Skyline Wesleyan Church featured, first in *Ten of the Most Innovative Churches*, presents this as his formula for change:

People change when they:

- Hurt enough that they want to change;
- Learn enough that they want to change;
- Receive enough that they are able to change.[16]

This formula can be applied to a congregation as well. Change occurs when members are hurt or dissatisfied, when they learn of better ways of doing ministry, or when they have become so identified with Christ's Great Commission that they feel compelled to help bring about needed changes. In *Twelve Keys to an Effective Church*, Callahan gives this as his first principle:

> Churches that have been effective in mission have tended to identify very specific human hurts and hopes with which they have shared their leadership and financial resources. Mission outreach does not come from planning retreats and board meetings; more often it starts because 3–5 people have a longing to help a specific human hurt and hope.[17]

Creating an Awareness of Need

For a need to become a driving force, it must be felt by all whose involvement is needed. The truth of this became apparent in one of our field experiments at Search Institute for the Institute of Mental Health. In carrying out our experiment, skilled consultants made personal visits to youth organizations to offer training in a highly respected program, free of charge. The program, known as Peer Helping, trained adults and youth in friendship skills. Search Institute offered to train representatives of these youth-serving organizations to become leaders of this program in their local organization. The usual charge for this training was several hundred dollars per person.

Knowing of the program's popularity and the high words of praise being given it by agency and congregational leaders, we puzzled over the fact that some groups accepted the offer with enthusiasm and others did not. To find possible reasons, we listened to audiotapes of the conversations that occurred when the offer was made.

Our first analysis was of tapes from the five groups that unanimously accepted the offer. We found the following pattern of response from these groups:

1. Linkage of need: Early in the visit, people begin to identify local needs with the innovative program, sharing experiences to illustrate the need.

2. *Tentative commitment:* Following the presentation, persons began to think out loud about specific dates, times, and places for taking the training.

3. *Expanding possibilities:* Ideas were given of how the innovative program could be used in their local program.

Motivating their comments were these factors: (1) previous success with innovations, (2) trust in the consultant, (3) high regard for the sponsoring organization.

An analysis of the taped conversation of the five groups rejecting the offer showed a mixed reaction to the worthwhileness of the consultant's visit. When answering the question "Did you consider this evening's visit valuable?", the answers varied among "somewhat," "not sure," or "no." Their halfhearted response and low enthusiasm over the offer showed that it did not address a deeply felt need.[18] (Further analysis provided additional evidence of the power found in a group's awareness of need.[19])

Though congregations can be conscious of many needs and can speak persuasively about them, a need to become a driving force must be felt, it must touch emotions, trouble consciences, and move people to action. When that happens, the requisite power to effect a significant change is unleashed.

A sense of need is powerful. This fact became evident in the patterned response of 2,693 adults in the Innovation Study when they answered items related to need. The consistency of their response caused the following items to intercorrelate and form a cluster we called Desire to Change (see sidebar 5.1). The items describe the compelling desire of some members to improve what is presently being done, a restiveness for action, and a strong motivation to get started.

The most convincing evidence of the power found in a sense of need became available when we revisited the agencies three years later. We found that groups (agencies, schools, or congregations) scoring high on Desire for Change in the first survey had become involved in carrying out a remarkable list of innovations during the intervening years. For instance, 4-H groups scoring high on this scale reported having designed new curriculum activities for, with, and by their members. Also, they told of having made special efforts to understand better not only the interests, goals, and concerns of their members but also those of families in their county. Similar reports did not occur for groups scoring low on this measure.

Similarly, during a three-year period, the Catholic and Jesuit schools showed a noteworthy response to meeting needs troubling to them. Those scoring high on Desire for Change differed from all other schools in the way they introduced innovative courses, such as electives addressing societal issues and remedial programs for incoming freshmen. Linked to the willingness of these schools to make changes was an increased sensitivity to unfinished agendas. For instance, observers in these schools noted the dissatisfaction of faculty and students over what was being taught regarding matters of justice. They noted also the increased number of students volunteering for a service activity.

Because a felt need is such an important inner drive, one of the first tasks when proposing a desired change is to intensify a group's sense of need for the proposed change. Ideally, this is done by beginning with a core group of members and helping them identify the need for a change. Once they have committed to bringing about a proposed change, the issue needs to be presented to the larger membership. An initial core group serves as an important ingredient in stimulating others to a sense of need. But steps must be taken to assure that their felt need also filters through a variety of groups within the church until there is a shared ownership.

When we speak of a strong commitment made by a core group, we use the words expressed by a member who said, "I'm sticking with this project until its launched, no matter what happens."

But how is this degree of personal commitment for a needed change generated within one's membership?

CREATING AN INNER PERSUASION

An inner persuasion to do something is enhanced when people see how the need is related to the church's mission. Needs appropriate to Christ's Great Commission can be of two kinds: those evident to everyone in the congregation and those not immediately evident. Trying to initiate changes in one's congregational program to meet the first type of need is, of course, much easier than to awaken a deep concern for needs not yet recognized or acknowledged.

Evident Needs

Evident needs are the needs of hurting people who are looking for help, the kind which a congregation can most easily understand and address. When a task force in my congregation presented a workable plan that would provide transitional housing for homeless families, the plan drew strong support and affirmation. Why? Because most members were troubled by the thought of homeless families trying to survive in our community. Such raw, heart-rending issues face almost every congregation today.

Another pastor featured in *Ten Most Innovative Churches* has based his ministry on responding to the pressing needs of today. Taking seriously the counsel of Robert Schuller, "Find a need and fill it, find a hurt and heal it," Pastor Dale Galloway has established over five hundred small groups in his congregation known as TLC (Tender, Loving Care). Members in this rapidly growing congregation, New Hope Community Church of Portland, Oregon, are dedicated to ministries that include support for alcohol- and drug-dependent persons, blended families, separated and divorced people, victims of rape, people with eating disorders, and many other similar groups. People who join the congregation are helped to become aware of the importance of this ministry and to become caregivers within the small group they join.

The value of letting needs shape the ministry of a congregation however, is a debatable issue for many pastors. In the report *Church Membership Initiative,* interviews of a national sample of parish pastors showed two distinct groups of religious leaders. One supported the point of view that the church must meet the needs of people. Those holding this viewpoint are in congregations that are growing.

The second group of pastors was hostile to this point of view, insisting that people's needs center only in a clear understanding of the law/gospel dynamic. Hence, they insist, a congregation's ministry should focus only on preaching and teaching God's Word. Those holding this viewpoint, however, were usually in small congregations that are not growing.

Most illuminating in the *Church Membership Initiative* report was the finding that a majority of congregations in the study showed little motivation to increase their membership. When asked about the value of membership growth, most would say they want growth. But contradicting this statement were their attitudes toward innovative activities necessary for growth. On such issues as establishing a mission statement; defining needs to be met; revising worship style; evaluating liturgy; and rethinking their programs, style of ministry, and the like, these people were consistently and overtly opposed to doing what fosters growth.[20] Though saying they want membership growth, they felt no need to make changes essential for reaching out to their community.

Such congregations lack an awareness of the basic reason for the church's existence: to help people who are outside the kingdom of God into a saving relationship with Jesus Christ. Lacking such a concern for the spiritual welfare of friends and neighbors, members are not likely to take seriously Christ's Great Commission to make disciples of all nations.

Needs that Are Not Evident

More difficult is the task of creating a compelling sense of concern for needs that are not evident to members. Such needs include a general lack of spiritual interest, an unwillingness to reach out to others, absence of a drive to serve, materialism, a law-oriented belief system, and acceptance of heretical beliefs. When information about hidden needs is made available, it sometimes is not taken seriously. People avoid messages that are in conflict with their preconceptions, a tendency called "selective exposure." Some people tend to see and hear only what fits their concept of where people are with respect to matters of faith and how a church should function.

To change the status quo of a congregation, members must have an inner persuasion of the need to change. Such a persuasion represents a far more powerful force than the external persuasion used by a congregation's leader. But how is this inner persuasion created when the deeper needs of people are not evident?

One effective way is to secure survey data that presents information on the values, beliefs, and attitudes of congregational members. Such information often surprises members. This is especially true when they see the discrepancy between what members believe, value, and do, and what is confessed each Sunday in the Creed and heard regularly in the pastor's sermons— namely, a gap between the congregation's functional theology and its professed beliefs.

The Effective Christian Education Study[21] provided especially provocative information for the six Protestant denominations in the study because it did the revolutionary thing of assessing evidences of faith. It identified the percentages of people who possess a mature faith. the sobering results showed that only 8 percent of the men ages 40 to 49 gave evidence of an integrated faith, in contrast to 43 percent of the women that age. An awareness of this deficit in congregational life would never have been known except through a survey of this type.

Another need the study underscored has to do with Sunday school teachers. The finding was that no more than 43 percent of those teaching elementary-grade children gave evidence of an integrated faith,.

I quizzed several groups of Lutherans as to where they thought their church would rank in the assessment of faith maturity involving the six major Protestant denominations. Their guesses always placed Lutherans in first or second place. You can imagine their surprise when they discovered that the faith maturity scores of their youth and adults ranked fifth.

At two conferences involving over one hundred pastors each, however, the reaction was different. Having presented the survey information with its sobering comparisons, I asked how many were surprised. A few raised their hands. When I asked how many were not surprised, many hands went up. When I asked why this response, several pastors simply answered, while pointing to their chest, "We just sensed this to be the case."

A carefully conducted survey provides documentation for needs sensed but not voiced. The needs are not discussed because visible evidence is lacking. But once information is available, discussion of the need can begin. That is what has happened in churches as a result of the Effective Christian Education Study. Information showing the relatively low percentages of members who possess a well-developed faith, once public, has now become a topic of both concern and widespread discussion.

Surfacing less evident information is important. When people are helped to see the disparity between what the Lord of the church asks of his people and what currently exists, an inner persuasion to act is engendered. And the greater the contrast between God's "ought" and the congregation's "is," the more compelling the sense of need. (Congregational surveys are available through Search Institute to assist in identifying these less evident needs.[22])

THE IDEAL AND THE REAL

When we talk about meeting needs related to the mission of the church, we invariably think in terms of goals or desired outcomes. That is natural because it is generally assumed that all organizations exist for goal-seeking purposes. That, however, has not always been true for the church.

Richard Hutcheson, who has had over thirty years of administrative experience in the Presbyterian church as pastor, chaplain, and presbytery executive, calls attention to an interesting fact. In *Wheel within the Wheel*, he points out that classical Christian thinking has viewed the church as existing "to be" and not "to do." His review of classical statements of the church, beginning with the early creeds and confessions, shows they never mention the goals, mission, or purpose of the church. Rather they focus only on what the church is to be—a people of God, a community of faith, the body of Christ.

Hutcheson notes however, that though its purpose has not been explicit in statements of the church, it has been implicit in its ministry. Congregations have sent out missionaries, established social service institutions, founded schools, provided for the poor, sponsored Sunday schools, and the like, even though they lacked a mission statement. As he points out, mission statements are a recent phenomenon in the life of any organization. A pre–1945 dictionary would probably define mission as the "act of sending" and connect the word with the church's missionary activity. It is only recently that the military concept of mission as a task to perform has been adopted by secular as well as religious organizations.[23]

Uniquely, a congregation's task is to determine what God is doing and wishes to do in the community being served. Knowing that Christ was concerned with the sick, hungry, imprisoned, lonely, and the lost of his day, members are reminded they need to be "little Christs" (Martin Luther's term) as they encounter need. In doing so they are operating as Christ's church because they are responding as his body. This response may be identified as an implicit sense of God's "ought" or God's agenda. These efforts to reach out could be called unstated but implicit goals. As such they are significant because they generate a feeling of concern when members see a great disparity between what they implicitly desire and the realities about them.

Implicit Goals

Most members in a congregation want to see their children grow up to become responsible adults whose lives are governed by knowledge of God's universal moral laws and God's love care, and are motivated by faith in Jesus Christ. These deeply held hopes and aspirations are seldom identified as goals of a congregation. Nevertheless, they operate as implicit goals.

In 1990, I was present at an invitational conference in St. Louis, where representatives from six major Protestant denominations met to study a report on the Effective Christian Education Study. The first evening Shelby Andress and I tabulated the reports from each denomination's thirty representatives about what concerned them most in the report. Ranking number one for all six denominations was their concern over the extent to which their high school youth were involved in at-risk behaviors. It is doubtful that any of these denominations have an explicit goal regarding the ethical and moral behavior of their youth. Yet the disparity between what these assembled Christian educators desire for their youth and what they saw could destroy their youth's future was most troubling. Needless to say, it motivated these denominational educators to take action to address this problem. An implicit goal became an explicit one for these Christian educators.

A similar sense of need resulted in a remarkable set of action steps for an entire church body. A conference held at Loma Linda, California, brought together the top officials of the Seventh-day Adventist Church, including the presidents of their thirteen colleges and universities. They listened and evaluated a report describing the condition of their much cherished, church-sponsored schools. They heard about the diminished faith and denominational loyalty of their students, the declining enrollments in many of their schools, and the specter of financial bankruptcies.

This report had serious implications for this small church body, because members view their 1,113 elementary schools, 94 academies (secondary schools), and 13 colleges as the way to perpetuate their denomination, the primary way to nurture and maintain the values and faith traditional to their church. Hence, concern gripped these leaders when data from a national survey of their people showed a marked decline in school enrollment, a relatively high percentage of their high school youth rebelling against the church and its regulations, and the likelihood of financial crisis for many of their schools.

Unspoken by these leaders was the strong desire that their youth embrace the Adventist faith and enroll in their schools, with parents underwriting the costs. The disparity between what they deemed ideal and what the survey showed as reality was most disturbing. The disparity created an inner persuasion to do something no denomination had previously done.

After deliberating over the data these seventy-five people resolved to launch a three-year project involving all aspects of their church, including local schools and congregations. The declared purpose of this massive effort, known as Project Affirmation, was to awaken concern in all parts of the church to their current situation and to stimulate discussion regarding what needed to be done. They established four task forces to address each of the most troubling aspects of the report: Youth and the Church, Parochial Teachers, Finances, and Marketing. Because these task forces (which met several times each year) wanted more information on issues relating to their youth, schools, and congregations, they launched the largest study of any single church body. They collected information from over twelve thousand parochial school youth in grades 6–12 using a survey instrument of three hundred items.

Peter Benson, president of Search Institute, unveiled the results of this massive study to assembled church officials and members of the two boards that launched the study. Church officials who had dragged their feet on cooperating with Project Affirmation now heard news that intensified their concern over the future of their church. They heard that youth reared in their schools perceived their congregations as cold and not open to discussion of important questions. Worse yet, they heard that these negative perceptions mounted as the youth approached their senior year in high school. And most sobering of all was the evidence showing how a works orientation was eroding youth's faith in Christ. It showed that the majority of their students believe that salvation depends on one's behavior instead of on what God has done. The church officials were not pleased to hear this. Nor were they pleased to learn that scores on Maturity of Faith for their twelve thousand youth did not advance from sixth grade to the senior year, even though the young people were in their parochial school system.

In a remarkable response to a sense of need created by this information, these church officials took action. First, they authorized the churchwide distribution of the report along with carefully stated recommendations addressing all levels of church life. In addition, they gave authorization for a series of innovations that centered on training programs, publications, new curricula, policy changes, and revised text books. The innovations they approved were designed by the four task forces that focused their efforts on needs made evident in previous studies and the new survey. Clearly they were motivated by information that highlighted a striking disparity between what they wanted for their youth and what they saw happening.

These two examples show how research information can serve to introduce dissatisfaction with the status quo. It can accomplish what has been long observed: "Discontented systems generally are more innovative than contented ones." And in reverse, "The more successful an organization is, the more likely it will continue to maintain the status quo and the less likely it is to change how it performs."

A Focus on Possibilities

Everett Rogers, in *Diffusion of Innovations,* makes an interesting observation: "An individual may develop a need when he or she learns that an innovation exists. Therefore, innovation can lead to needs as well as vice versa."[24] To see Rogers's observation in action, one need only visit the many churches that have introduced changes in their method of ministry because their pastor attended a workshop in which Robert Schuller told of what he is doing.

To illustrate, my congregation was interviewing a candidate for the position of senior pastor. In the course of the interview, the candidate told about the many refugees his congregation on the West Coast had welcomed and given housing and support. The example he gave of his congregation and the blessing it had been to his people awakened interest among members in our congregation. As a result they took on a similar innovation of welcoming refugees, a project that brought a great deal of blessing to many. One member, for instance, welcomed four young Vietnamese boat people into his home. Later, he and his wife adopted two of the youngsters as their own. One became a medical doctor and for a time was in Vietnam providing medical help to refugees, such as he had been.

One can wonder, Does a need precede knowledge of a new idea or does knowledge of an innovation create a need for that new idea?[25] This much is for sure. The pastor who wishes to encourage a congregation to be responsive to human need does well to expose members to the many innovative ministries being launched by congregations around the country. Workshops, conferences, publications, and videos all serve to awaken people to new possibilities and potentials.

A feeling of obligation to act can also arise out of heightened awareness of certain strengths in ones' congregation. An outstanding choral or drama group can become involved in witness activities through public performances. An exceptional program of recruiting and training adults to serve as teachers in a Christian Education program can motivate a congregation to consider sharing what they have learned.

First Lutheran Church in Duluth, Minnesota, energized by what they saw happening in their congregation, conducted workshops on Christian education in various parts of the state. Pleasure and joy over the results of their program created a sense of need to share what they had learned with other congregations. Kennon

Callahan stresses this point. Base your long-range plans on what you do well, he says, on your strengths.

This much seems clear: A sense of need—an inner persuasion that changes are needed—is essential. It comes when a consciousness of what God wants to accomplish through a congregation is seen in juxtaposition to a clear picture of what is not being done. Posing such contrasts serves the purpose of generating a creative tension.

A creative tension follows when the vision people have for their congregation becomes a calling rather than just a good idea. For them the goals of a congregation are never achieved. There is always a disparity between the "is" and the "ought." There is never a time when these people can say, "We have arrived." They are always wondering how they can more fully live out the mission of Jesus Christ and draw on the power in his promises.

Inasmuch as members of a congregation are likely to become aware of a plethora of needs, a basis is needed for determining what is appropriately a congregational ministry. The next chapter deals with this issue by showing that the needs to be addressed are those that relate to the mission and values of a congregation.

Reflection:
Becoming Aware of Needs

• Does our congregation have survival needs similar to those of Lone Wolf or Tri-County?

• How might we adopt a listening stance to become more aware of community needs?

• What are some community needs our congregation could address now?

• What are some congregational needs people sense?

• How might we motivate people to act on needs in our community or congregation?

CHAPTER SIX

TIE INNOVATIONS TO MISSION AND VALUES

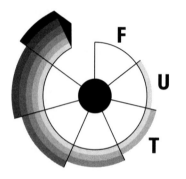

"Values are the 'mental models' that shape how we act. They provide the prism through which all behavior is ultimately viewed."

—*Peter Senge*

PASTOR JOY JOHNSON is pastor of Bethlehem Lutheran Church, an inner-city congregation of 425 members in St. Paul, Minnesota. Seeing that her church is increasingly surrounded by a muticultural population of Hmongs, various ethnic blacks, and Asians, she has fostered a sense of mission to the community. This value-orientation became evident when thirty-six members gathered on two evenings for a Vision-to-Action workshop.

Once they had reviewed survey material describing their external and internal environment, the members proceeded to write scenarios of what they would like to see happening three years hence. What they wrote classified into eleven different categories, most of which were oriented to outreach in the community. The classification of scenarios included the following:

- varieties of inspiring worship
- service to the community
- resources for family problems and issues
- making everyone feel welcome
- youth and adults cooperating in service
- a Wednesday-night, multicultural education event
- interactive educational opportunities
- intergenerational faith sharing

Faced with security issues and a membership that no longer lives in the community, the group decided on using a Wednesday-night series of activities to address many of their hopes and dreams. They designed an evening that begins with a meal, after which participants fan out for choristers, confirmation instruction, Bible study and discussion, instruction in home and car repair, crafts, story time, and adult choir. The group is thrilled because the evening is attracting volunteers, members, and people from outside their membership.

When the community became traumatized by five shootings and a death within blocks of the church, as well as by growing evidence of crass racial discrimination, Bethlehem sponsored a day of reconciliation that included people of different faiths, ethnic backgrounds, and churches. The well-publicized event set in motion a series of block parties at which people came together to promote unity and a sense of community solidarity. An excellent beginning is being made by this congregation that decided to stay in a deteriorating community and view their neighborhood as a mission field.

VALUES AND ORGANIZATIONS

Every organization has a culture shaped by values established over time that reflect the values of its leaders, opinion makers, and founders. That is true for colleges, schools, health centers, medical schools, youth organizations, service agencies, and especially congregations. Each has dominant values that reflect its sense of mission, its defenses, and cultural norms. These values operate profoundly to shape or strongly influence the decisions made and directions taken.

Notice what several writers have to say about the shaping power of values. James Kouzes and Barry Posner, business consultants for organizational development at San Jose University, write:

> Values are deep-seated standards that influence almost every aspect of our lives: our moral judgments, our responses to others, our commitments to personal and organizational goals. However silently, values give direction to the hundreds of decisions made at all levels of an organization. Options that run counter to the group's value system are seldom considered. Values constitute our personal bottom line.[1]

Peter Senge refers to values as "mental models" that shape how we act. They provide the prism through which all behavior is ultimately viewed. Though people may not act in a way that is congruent with the theory or theology they espouse, they do behave in a manner congruent with their functional theology or theory-in-use (their mental model). Such models are powerful because they affect what we see. "Two people with different mental models can observe the same event and describe it differently because they have looked at different details." Mental models or values shape perception.[2]

The problem with values is that they often exist below our level of awareness, rising only to be articulated or to feed our emotions when an activity is seen as incompatible with the value. In times of conflict, a person's pattern of values become apparent. They dictate a person's behavior.

This topic of mission and values is an important one for those whose business it is to teach values so they become internalized. It is appropriate to encourage church members to ponder, "Is what we confess every Sunday truly one of my values? Is it part of my vision?" The questions are important because a value is not a governing value until it has become an inner mental image that guides one's perceptions and behavior. Therefore, the task of congregational leaders is to help people internalize the kind of values that lead them to become little Christs to a lost world.

But how are values made real in a congregation? One way is through people's behavior and actions, not least through what is said by leaders of the congregation. "Every action that a leader takes or doesn't take is information about the leader's values and the seriousness with which they are held."[3]

Tying innovation to mission and values is vital. To instill values associated with progress and tie them to proposed innovations is a basic task. It involves helping members form a shared vision that connects with their own personal visions for the congregation. When a shared vision becomes compelling and engaging, members begin to feel personally responsible for making the vision happen.

FOCUSING ON YOUR MISSION

According to the Innovation Study, the most powerful predictor of a readiness to respond, is valuing one's organizational mission, the "why we exist." Therefore, to link an innovation from the beginning to the congregation's mission is to encourage broad acceptance and support.

When Pastor Linda Grounds was serving Randolph United Methodist Church, a rural congregation of eighty-three members from Minneapolis, Minnesota, she wanted to introduce tithing as a congregational norm. To do this she linked the innovation to the congregation's purpose. "The purpose of the church is not just to exist, to sustain itself," she emphasized. "The purpose of the church is to change the world."

She suggested Randolph United Methodist Church start tithing as a congregation so they would have more money to give away for ministries such as helping a mother on welfare learn a profession, or sending money to a Twin Cities shelter for the homeless. These funds would be given over and above what they gave to the Methodist Conference's annual appropriation for mission endeavors.

The proposed innovation caused members to realize they needed to put God first in their lives. They needed to let go of their attachment to money and trust that God would provide for them. According to Martha Sawyer Allen, writer of a news article about this congregation, a new norm has been adopted. It is the one espoused in Malachi 3:10. "Bring the whole tithe into the storehouse. . . . Test me in this," says the Lord Almighty, "and see if I will not throw open the floodgates of heaven and pour out so much blessing that you will not have room enough for it."

Now the congregation pays its pastor on time, maintains its church and parsonage, upgrades its facilities on occasion, and sends its full obligation to the national denomination. In addition, money is available for acts of mercy and service.[4]

A Congregational Sense of Mission

In the congregations participating in the Innovation Study, those whose adult leaders placed a high value on Sense of Mission showed over a three-year period an impressive number of progressive activities, all related to the mission of a congregation. Here are some of the youth-oriented activities that appeared only in these congregations.

• Youth, staff, volunteers, and adult leaders were all involved in some form of leadership training.
• The youth participated in activities designed to effect needed changes in their organization.
• A high percentage of the youth participated in weekend retreats.
• The youth spoke of their work experiences as opportunities to serve as well as earn money.
• The youth exhibited a concern for people.[5]

These items suggest an underlying sense of mission, an awareness of the reason their youth group was in existence.

When I served as national youth director for a Lutheran denomination, I was impressed by the sense of mission that motivated a small youth group in Silverton, Oregon. Though lacking a youth director and a pastor who was particularly "good with youth," the fifteen or so young people reflected the value orientation of their homes. With their gifts of songs and witness, they visited hospitals, nursing homes, and churches. When they graduated from high school and moved on to college, several of them brought their strong sense of mission to the campus of Willamette University. Here they helped form a Bible study group that viewed the campus, including faculty, as their mission field.

Their first focus was on a political science professor who had been challenging them to be open to various political viewpoints. They adopted his stance by challenging him likewise to be open to the claims of the Christian faith. He accepted their challenge, including an invitation to attend their Bible studies. The result was that this political science professor, Mark Hatfield, became a Christian. Later, as a distinguished senator from Oregon, Mark Hatfield acknowledged publicly that this group of mission-oriented young people was responsible for his conversion.

People with a strong sense of mission (as typified by this youth group) tend to evaluate new proposals in terms of how an innovation will advance the mission of their organization. The kinds of questions they are inclined to ask form the cluster in sidebar 6.1. These items are criteria some adult leaders use when evaluating a proposed program for their youth.

These questions tend to be asked silently by those who have a strong sense of mission. That is what happened when people in the Innovation Study responded to these items scattered throughout the questionnaire. Their unique pattern of response caused the items to intercorrelate and form the cluster in the sidebar.

Significantly, parochial schools where faculty identified strongly with these items showed an impressive burst of innovative activity over the following three year period. Observers of these National Catholic Education Association schools noted their special sensitivity to the spiritual development of lay faculty and the school's growth as a Christian community. Their innovative activities addressed areas of school life they believed had been neglected.

Mission-oriented Jesuit schools in the study adopted new and more spontaneous forms of worship during the three-year period. Their feeling that they needed to serve the larger community resulted in a requirement that every student participate in some service activity. Importantly, we found a strong association between the mission orientation of groups in the Innovation Study and their launching of activities to enhance the spiritual purpose of either church or school.

SIDEBAR 6.1
Scale 7: Focusing on Mission
(A group evaluates a proposed program)

- Does it relate to a high priority goal?
- Does it fit into the total program?
- Is it based on an analysis of needs to be met?
- Is enthusiasm high for the proposed program among staff and/or volunteers?
- Will it make positive changes in the lives of people?
- Do I personally believe in it?

The Importance of Mission

Why is it so important that members come to understand and value the mission of their congregation? Because then they can begin to connect that mission with their own personal sense of purpose. This connection enhances motivation, commitment, and a general sense of fulfillment. Enlightened leaders of business are very aware of this. They spend time developing a corporate mission they want their employees to understand and value.[6] Peters and Waterman wrote, "Every excellent company we studied is clear on what it stands for and takes the process of value seriously. In fact, we wonder whether it is possible to be an excellent company without clarity on values and without having the right sort of values."[7]

Kouzes and Posner add, "People want to make a commitment to a purpose, a goal, a vision that is bigger than themselves. One of the best kept secrets in America is that people are aching to make a commitment—if only they had the freedom and the environment in which to do so."[8]

What these leaders in the business world have to say applies even more to the church. Note for instance this comment by Laura Spencer, developer of the Top Strategic Planning Process used in developing nations and multinational corporations. "Every organization, every social movement begins with a dream. The dream is the force that invents the future. Regardless of what we call it, there is a desire to make something happen, to change the way things are."[9]

A Theology of Mission

According to Richard Hutcheson, it is impossible to adopt organizational insights from business management without adopting their underlying assumption, namely, that organizations exist to achieve goals. The danger implicit in adopting this assumption is that the church is made human-centered rather than God-centered. Furthermore, it runs counter to the traditional concept of the church. The church exists not to do something but to be something, namely, a people of God, a community of faith, the body of Christ.[10]

One need only think of the Lutheran description of a congregation. "A congregation is where the Word of God is preached and the sacraments rightly administered." Without question many pastors feel their responsibility ends once they had preached God's Word and administered the sacraments. Because they believe God does it all, some resist outreach efforts, even those efforts that seem to be a natural response to Christ's command, "Go and make disciples of all nations." Some clergy resisted first efforts to establish a foreign mission or to adopt Sunday schools, or embrace youth organizations.

The most striking passage that seems to counter the idea that the church is only to "be" rather than "do" is found in Matthew 25. Here Christ describes a judgment scene in which the goats are separated from the sheep on the basis of one criterion—what they did or did not do for their less fortunate brothers and sisters.

Truth is found in the following dialectic: We are called to be God's people, totally dependent on him and his providential intervention. At the same time, we are called to do—to make disciples, to show mercy, to live as responsible citizens. Our task is to maintain the tension of being both dependent on God's intervention (God-centered) and wise as serpents (human-centered). We are to learn from one another how best to serve as little Christs.

Many congregations have no sense of mission. They have become, as Lyle Schaller observes, "directionless." They tend to redefine their purpose in terms of institutional maintenance and survival. The care and feeding of the organization, rather than service to constituencies, is their number one priority. For some churches the pull toward a goalless existence is enhanced by frequent pastor turnover, entrenched lay leadership, and long-established traditions. For such congregations reevaluation of purpose and the development of new goals is most difficult.[11]

But it is still true that a visionary pastor can awaken a directionless congregation to a sense of purpose and mission that transforms the members. *Marketing for Congregations* tells the story of Bethel African Methodist Episcopal Church, located in a low-income area of Baltimore.[12] In 1975 the congregation was stagnant: only half of its six hundred members were attending Sunday services. That was before John Bryant, age thirty-two, arrived with dreams of what a city church could do. Pastor Bryant envisioned a church that would reach out to the whole person and the surrounding community.

The authors provide the following account:

> Among the church programs started were sign language instruction for about 50 deaf parishioners; a prison missionary project for adults and youth; an outreach that provides job counseling, clothing, food, and vouchers for emergency payment of rent and utility bills; an energy cooperative that sells fuel oil at reduced prices; and a 2,000 member food cooperative. The Senior Citizens Eating Together programs serve free meals to members and non-members alike.

Yet the religious message of this congregation was not forgotten. In addition to three Sunday services, Bethel sponsors Sunday school classes for all ages plus daily Bible classes and discussion groups. Bryant's spirit has spread to his congregants, one of whom gave money to start a ministry for cancer patients and their families—a program that several other churches have copied. By 1984 membership had climbed to 6,000 with a paid staff of 31 and dozens of volunteers. As one church member noted, "We're not just adding people to the church rolls. Reverend Bryant has shaken our consciousness and awakened us as Christians."[12]

Churches in Mission

Kennon Callahan, whose life work has been consulting with congregations, believes the day of the churched culture and the professional pastor is over. The day of the mission field and the missionary pastor has come. "Our current problems have more to do with mission than membership, more with service than survival, more with the planet than the church plant, more with the human hurts and hopes of the world than the hemorrhaging of a denomination." For him, the day of the local church is over. The day of the mission outpost has come.[13]

A striking example of what Callahan has in mind is found in the sense of mission that has characterized the ministry of Pastor Rick Warren. He and the seven members of the new Saddleback Community Church determined that their mission would be this: "We will be a church for the unchurched 'Saddleback Sam,'" the unchurched yuppie living in Saddleback Valley in South California. He came to this sense of mission after conducting a marketing study of Saddleback Valley. He conducted a door-to-door survey in the vicinity of his home, during which he visited with more than 500 residents. From the results of his survey he developed a philosophy of ministry that centered on these elements:

1. Saddleback Church would be a church for people who did not like to go to church. They would focus on baby boomers who are interested in spiritual values but believe the church has little or nothing to say about spiritual things.
2. The operating style of the church would be open, friendly, unstructured, and nonbureaucratic.
3. The services would be informal, in keeping with the southern California lifestyle.

The entire weekend program is designed to communicate to the unchurched and uncommitted. The midweek services, on the other hand, are designed to communicate with those who have accepted the church's message and are committed to growth and maturity in their religious journey.[14]

The congregation of seven has grown to an average Sunday attendance of 6,000. His first public service attracted 205 in 1980. Twelve years later, on Easter Sunday 1992, more than 14,000 were in attendance. The congregation has founded twenty other congregations, whose pastors meet monthly as a support group. When interviewed by the authors of *Marketing for Congregations* in 1992, the church's leaders identified their five constituencies: a core ministry group of approximately 1,000 people; a group of 1,900 people committed to maturity in the Christian life; a committed membership of 2,400; Sunday attenders varying in number from 4,500 to 7,000 on a given Sunday; and a community of 16,000 occasional attenders.

The authors of *Marketing for Congregations*, who supplied the information given above, identify four questions a congregation should consider when formulating a mission statement. These questions help members arrive at an understanding of what God is calling them to be and to do at a particular time.

1. What does Scripture and our own faith tradition tell us about our mission?
2. What unique and specific needs and interests do our members want the congregation and its programs to satisfy?

3. What specific needs in our community can and should we address?

4. What specific needs in society and the world can and should we address?

Noting the tendency of congregations to focus on one or the other of these questions, the authors insist that all four should be held in tension if a congregation is to correctly understand its mission. In making explicit its mission a congregation should identify its target population (Who is to be served?), the needs to be addressed (What is to be satisfied?), and the services to be offered (How are people's needs to be met?).

Ideally, the formulators of the mission statement, when seeking to meet the above criteria, should focus on: (1) what is feasible for their congregation to attempt, (2) what is distinctive, distinguishing them from neighboring congregations, and (3) what will motivate members with a sense of being involved in something worthwhile.[15]

Mission statements that meet the guidelines presented above will provide the congregation's focus and define what it should seek to do and be. Once formulated by core members of the congregation, a mission statement can become a statement of what is valued most. It will encourage a shared desire that nothing be allowed to interfere with the mission. "Let us throw off everything that hinders and the sin that so easily entangles, and let us run with perseverance the race marked out for us" (Hebrews 12:1).

EXPECTING RESULTS

With a clear sense of mission come expectations that good will come in the future, lives will be changed and people will benefit. This is about "hope"—a faith directed toward the future. It is not an abstract idea but a picture of what is to be sought. If mission defines *why* a congregation exists, vision identifies *what* is to be sought or realized in the future.

Expecting results means members of the congregation have a vision they take seriously, a vision focused on a specific destination, a future they seek to create. It is their vision of what can happen that leads them to claim the promises of God, to expect through a faith activated by prayer to move mountains.

The vision is a shared one when members have a similar picture of what is desired and are bound together by a common aspiration to see it become a reality. It is more than an idea; it is a force in people's hearts, a force of impressive power.[16]

In *Without a Vision, the People Perish*, George Barna defines this vision as "a clear mental image of a preferable future, imparted by God to His chosen servants, based upon an accurate understanding of God, self, and circumstances." He calls it "a picture held in your mind's eye of the way things could or should be in the days ahead. Vision connotes a visual reality, a portrait of conditions that do not currently exist." The purpose of a vision is not to acquiesce to a future handed down but to create the future.[17]

Bill Hybels, pastor of Willow Creek Community Church in South Barrington, Illinois, had a vision of reaching the "Unchurched Harrys and Marys" of the baby boom generation, those who see the church as irrelevant, stodgy, boring, and predictable. To bring his vision into being, he and his staff make sure that their church is anything but irrelevant, stodgy, and boring. Intent on seeing this vision become a reality, they have been successful in reaching their target audience. Today the church welcomes over fourteen thousand to its seeker-targeted worship services.

The power in a vision, in dreaming about the future, is seen in the findings of Kirk Hadaway's 1988 study of five hundred metropolitan Southern Baptist churches. His sample included three kinds of congregation: those that were growing, those that had plateaued, and those that were declining in membership. He found that pastors in 54 percent of the Growing Churches say their members lean toward "dreaming about the future" rather than "living in the past." This compares to only 21 percent of those in Plateaued Churches and 15 percent of those in Declining Churches. In Growing Churches, he finds, members are not satisfied with the status quo. They want to reach others with the gospel and feel their church can do a better job of it.[18]

This value of having a vision and wanting it to happen represents a type of restiveness with the status quo, a desire to see movement toward a hoped-for outcome. It is a value orientation found among enough people to have created the cluster in sidebar 6.2.

Congregations in our study that placed a high value on these items showed one distinctive aspect: They did creative things during their three-year period.

Originating the Vision

The pastor may be the originator of the vision. This is best done through sermons that describe possibilities, convey a sense of urgency, and draw attention to the spiritual growth linked to pioneer endeavor. Studies of growing churches show that it is not any particular type of preaching content or style that makes the difference in growing congregations but rather preaching that awakens visions of what God can be doing through God's servants.

A vision becomes a living force when people truly believe they can, with God's help, shape the future. For people of faith this confidence is God-given, the result of asking God, who has all authority and power, to intervene. This joining together in prayer results in members being joined not only to a larger purpose but also to one another. This connectedness helps keep the vision alive.

For many in the congregation, however, there is no vision, no sense of what the church wants to see happen, no picture of a desired future.

One year I was involved in developing a survey instrument called Shared Vision. Its purpose was to provide a way for members of a congregation to rank the importance of forty goal statements and evaluate how well these goals were being achieved in their congregation. When pilot testing the survey, I invited a group of people to my home to react to the items and critique them.

What impressed me was the interest this process generated in the group. Instead of leaving at the time I promised they could go, they stayed twice as long. Why? One put into words what the others were thinking: "These goal statements tell me something I had not known before—what the goals of a congregation are or might be." He had no vision, no sense of what the goals of his congregation were.

At Augsburg Youth and Family Institute, we present seven basic visions that might be sought over time by teachers, parents, and staff of a congregation. Each represents a dream that youth of the congregation by the time they graduate from high school, may have come to:

- know Christ
- understand grace
- be interested in Scripture
- know self-esteem
- be unprejudiced
- be mission oriented
- be involved in service activities

These results ought to be part of every congregation's desired future. A denominational educator said it well, "If we cannot save our own youth, how can we as a church save the world for Christ?"

The Importance of Prayer

A highly significant intersection between the human and divine takes place through prayer. Prayer is a way of arriving at a vision of what is important to God, members of the congregation, and people in the community. It is a way of undergirding all human efforts being made in the congregation with the spiritual power needed to bring each vision into being.

Consider the goal and vision orientation of the following passage: "If two of you on earth agree about anything you ask for, it will be done for you by my Father in heaven" (Matthew 18:19). Consider also the widow Christ used as an example of how we should pray. She pestered the unjust judge out of a strong desire to reach her goal until he, weary of her entreaties, acquiesced simply to get rid of her. She pressed for results and that is how Christ asks us to pray (Luke 11:5-10).

I visited a small, Korean Disciples of Christ congregation with 132 members because its members had ranked especially high on the assessment of faith maturity. This small congregation in Chicago, Illinois, reports between two and ten adult baptisms each year.

What impressed me was the place of prominence given to Bible study and prayer, a tradition brought from Korea. Kai Cho Lee, a native of Korea who accompanied me on my two-day visit to this congregation, underscored this fact. She remembers her widowed mother rising for prayer and Bible study each morning from 4 to 6 A.M. After working all day to earn money for groceries and to raise eight children, she ended the day with another hour of prayer.

I found this disciplined approach to prayer also a characteristic of this congregation. The diminutive eighty-two-year-old grandmother of Pastor Soongook Choi had a daily routine that included two hours of prayer each morning and two hours each night. This strong accent on Bible study and prayer may account for the amazing growth of churches in Korea.

INSISTING ON QUALITY

To our surprise, placing a high value on quality, on doing things well, ranked second in predictive power of the twenty dimensions isolated in the Innovation Study. It was second only to Sense of Mission. People who placed a high value on quality might be described as cautious and deliberate. They wait and see what works well for others before adopting it themselves. Over time, however, they emerge as being progressive and responsive to challenge. Where quality is valued, good things tend to occur and progress becomes evident over time.

The Innovative Power of Valuing Quality

The Effective Christian Education Study, designed to determine which factors—originating in home or church—contributed most to the faith of members considered some one hundred factors. High quality Christian education emerged as the most potent factor, outranked only by a life-shaping Christian home.

Confirmation of this finding comes also from Hadaway. He found that adult Sunday schools were rated excellent or good in

84 percent of the Growing Churches, 56 percent of the Plateaued Churches, and in only 46 percent in the Declining Churches. This suggests that quality in Christian education is clearly linked not only with growth in maturity of faith but also with growth in church membership.

Other aspects of church life also show the importance of holding out for quality. Take, for instance, music in a worship service. Hadaway found that "a full 90% of large Growing Churches rate their music program as excellent or good, as compared to 78% of Plateaued Churches and 53% of Declining Churches. Among smaller churches, 65% of the Growing Congregations rate their music program as excellent or good, as compared to 37% of Plateaued Churches and 35% of Declining Churches." Obviously, a strong relationship exists for large and small churches between growth and quality of their music program.

Another example has to do with having worship services that are joyful, expectant and celebrative. Sixty percent of the Growing Churches say that this "always" or "usually" typifies their worship services, in contrast to 26 percent of the Plateaued Churches and 22 percent of the Declining Churches.[19] No wonder Kennon Callahan emphasizes the need for quality in planning, in the leading of liturgy, in preaching, and in singing by the choir. An emphasis on quality becomes literally one's offering or sacrifice to God as an organization. "You also, like living stones, are being built into a spiritual house to be a holy priesthood, offering spiritual sacrifices acceptable to God through Jesus Christ" (1 Peter 2:5).

Though the items in our survey were designed for both church and secular groups, the five that clustered around the construct Insisting on Quality adequately demonstrate that there are people who place a special value on high quality. The evidences they look for when evaluating a proposed innovation are listed in sidebar 6.3.

Note how a deliberate innovativeness is reflected in these items to suggest that fewer innovations but ones that last longer will be made. A striking example of this surfaced when we singled out two schools from the thirty randomly selected parochial schools of the National Catholic Educational Association. We chose the school scoring highest on our measure of Readiness for Change (School A) and the school scoring lowest (School B). The contrast between these two schools was dramatic. The first (we found out later) had a waiting list of students and a superb reputation whereas the other had a declining enrollment, low public image, and was teetering near bankruptcy.

The faculty at School B knew that changes were needed, things were not going well, and improvements needed to be made in their educational program. Hence responding to the item, "Our school is highly respected in the community," only 14 percent of the faculty agreed (in contrast to 93 percent of the faculty at School A). To the item, "I hear enthusiastic comments about our program from the people we serve," only 21 percent of the faculty at School B could agree (in contrast to 87 percent of the faculty at School A).

One difference between these two schools centered in the faculty's sense of mission. The contrast can be seen in the percentage of the two faculties who responded positively to the following items.

- Suppose you thought a given program would tap an unused potential in youth. Would you be very much influenced toward adopting it?

> School A: 73 percent   School B: 14 percent

- Suppose you thought a program would make positive changes in the lives of some youth. Would you be influenced very much toward the adoption of the program?

> School A: 73 percent   School B: 29 percent

Here are two schools whose sense of mission was poles apart. And significantly, one has a waiting list of students wishing to enroll and the other lacks students. School A initiated few but lasting innovations. School B, on the other hand, initiated many abortive, ill-conceived attempts to change and finally gave up.

An unexpected discovery in the Innovation Study was that an organization's innovativeness is highly dependent on the value orientation of its core members. We found that agencies and congregations whose people were united in a focus on mission distinguished themselves by doing remarkably innovative, mission-oriented things. And the more united they were in wanting all three of the following values, the more likely was their involvement in an innovative activity:

- a focus on mission
- an expectation of results (vision)
- an insistence on quality

We found the strongest predictors of innovativeness of all twenty factors were these three organizational values. They outrank in potency such factors as style of leadership, desire of members to see things change, resistance barriers, and group skills of members. This means congregations whose core members incarnate these value orientations will evidence notable progress toward achieving their mission. The implication is clear. If you as congregational leader wish to see your congregation respond to the challenge of the day, to the needs of a lost and suffering generation, you will do well to foster these three power-laden values.

Significantly, the pastor plays a key role by modeling these values. When an innovative program is being considered, it is the pastor's role to ask the question: "How will this innovation advance the values and mission of our congregation?" The question is key.

A unique force is embedded in congregations whose members have internalized a common purpose. Hence, tying an innovation or vision to this common purpose both reinforces a group's sense of mission and significantly increases the likelihood of support. People need to see the linkage between an innovation and the congregation's values when the innovation is presented to various constituencies and their approval and support is sought.

Reflection:
On Our Mission and Values

• Can members identify the mission of your congregation in one sentence?

• What do you see as your congregation's mission?

• What outcomes are desired most by leaders in your congregation?

• What innovations do you believe would advance the mission of your congregation?

• To what degree do you think high quality is valued and encouraged in your congregation? To what degree is prayer valued and encouraged?

CHAPTER SEVEN

USE THE INPUT OF LEGITIMIZERS

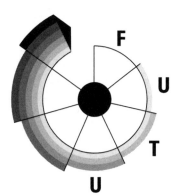

"Success is positively related to the extent that one works through opinion leaders."

—*Everett Rogers*

LEGITIMIZERS ARE THE GATEKEEPERS in a congregation, the people whose approval and support are needed if a change is to be made. Legitimizers include not only the pastor and formally elected leaders of a congregation but also the unofficial opinion makers whose position on a matter is influential. People who have status in the congregation and whose opinion is followed can be viewed as legitimizers.

Any task force intent on launching a laudable and much desired innovation, may wish to bypass legitimizers. The task force might view dealing with legitimizers as delaying the entire process. Someone might ask, "Why take time to involve legitimizers? They will only ask delaying questions and throw cold water on our good ideas." The task force is right in assuming there will be questions. Ronald Lippitt, a master in group leadership, said it well:

> It is typical and normal for there to be questioning of the validity and feasibility of new ideas, policies, regulations, procedures and programs. This questioning represents a natural and

potentially constructive resource for those responsible for change efforts. In fact, if there is no questioning it is probably a symptom of an unhealthy state of affairs where inhibitions and fears keep the questionings and feelings underground.[1]

Convinced of its vision to bring about an important innovation, a task force can easily view the process of fielding questions as time consuming and seemingly unnecessary. As a young pastor, that was my view. I would shy away from such procedures, choosing rather to barge ahead with changes that I deemed important and right.

In my first parish, I was aware of a large area north of our town, Mora, Minnesota, that had only one small church. When visiting some of the homes in this area, I discovered that many would like to have seen their children attend our Sunday school but lacked transportation or interest in providing it. It seemed obvious that if our church had a bus, we could bring these children to our church.

When in Duluth, Minnesota, I met a man who had an old school bus that he would sell for $300. Without having discussed the idea with any of my parishioners or church board, I agreed to the purchase saying, "If the bus will run from Duluth to Mora [about one hundred miles], we will assume it is in adequate running order. The money will be forthcoming when the bus arrives."

Not until I returned to Mora did I seek out a board member and ask that $300 be secured for payment if the bus was delivered in adequate shape. My failure to involve our church board could have led to my being tarred, feathered and run out of town.

But the lesson I learned came later when a board member faced me with this question: "Strommen, don't you think that it would be better if you discussed these things with your board before going ahead and doing them?" I realize now how ignorant I was of the importance of following procedures. I had not involved my congregation's legitimizers and given them the satisfaction of helping launch a significant innovation.

THE REALITY OF RESISTANCE

Chapter 2 posed the question, "Why is it so hard to introduce change?" It then identified the many factors that serve as obstacles and delaying factors in bringing about needed change. Because of the power of these factors, Benjamin and Walz, two social scientists at the University of Michigan, claim that a time frame of three to four years is needed for significant change.

Proposals to develop new programs or move one's organization in a new direction will always be resisted by some people. One of the most frequently found generalizations regarding resistance is this: "Resistance occurs when those affected by the change perceive it as threatening." Two other fundamental generalizations are: "People resist changes they do not understand"; and "People resist being forced to change."[3] That is why the support of legitimizers is so important.

A task force can expect at least three kinds of mild resistance: (1) skepticism over anything new, (2) defensiveness about the current situation, and (3) satisfaction with the status quo.

Resistance of these types has positive value. Those who are proposing a change are required to give more careful thought and preparation for the idea because of the resistance. The resistance of hard-to-convince people forces the task force to look carefully at the pros and cons of what is being proposed. It compels them to probe and examine facets of an innovation that might yield negative outcomes.

Skepticism about Anything New

This attitude, which a task force will meet, assumes that change is not needed in one's congregation. It is reflected in the seemingly insignificant questions, such as those in sidebar 7.1, hard-to-convince people tend to ask when something new is proposed.

The construct underlying these seemingly harmless and natural questions is resistance. It is seen in the fact that groups favoring these items are foot-draggers on any proposed innovation.

SIDEBAR 7.1
Scale 10: Hesitant Attitudes
(Reactions to a new program)

- I wonder who originated the new program.
- I wonder what others think about the new program.
- I wonder how the new program affects my area of responsibility.

For instance, those parochial schools where many tend to ask such questions are the schools, we found, that avoid giving raises to their faculty, doing long-range planning, conducting a curriculum review, selecting courses based on student needs, and the like.[4]

The three simple questions that form the scale Hesitant Attitudes are the visible tip of an iceberg of resistance that cannot be ignored. Hesitation is a subtle force that can deter a group from responding quickly to necessary changes. Other questions, equally harmless, could be substituted to indicate the same quality of resistance. Clearly, questions of this sort need to be anticipated and answered candidly.

Protecting One's Current Situation

A second, quite separate form of resistance is seen in the fear that any innovation will add responsibility or additional work. The resistance is created by feeling overcommitted in terms of time and energy. This sensitivity is expressed in items such as those listed in sidebar 7.2.

This protectiveness tends to be found in groups with traditional policies and practices. It is reflected in the activities characterizing parochial schools that favor these self-protection items. Such schools, we found, avoid innovative activities such as: establishing curricular advisory groups, reviewing resources available for meeting student needs, developing strategized methods of communicating with constituencies, or selecting courses that focus on clearly defined student needs. On the contrary, they characteristically retain traditional practices long discarded by sister schools.

SIDEBAR 7.2
Scale 11: Self Protection.
(People react to workload changes)

- I wonder whether the new assignments will mean a higher level of responsibility for me.
- I wonder whether a criticism of our current efforts is implied.
- I am suspicious of an idea if I distrust the presenter.
- I think of what must be given up if we adopt something new.
- I would be uneasy if I thought an idea could fail.

This resistance, however, can be a temporary one, encouraged by excessive workloads. We noticed that some of the schools described above did make innovative changes after three years. This suggests that this resistance, which a task force can expect, may dissipate if the issue of overloading is adequately addressed.

Contentment with the Status Quo

Present in every human service organization are people who psychologically resist anything new. It is an irrational but real response. They are satisfied with how things are going and are ready to say, "If it ain't broke, don't fix it." Often they are unwilling to see that something is "broke." Their contentment with status quo is reflected in limited horizons and a feeling that all is going well. In the Innovation Study, we found this form of resistance exists in sufficient strength to have caused a number of items to intercorrelate and form scale 12, Preference for the Status Quo, shown in sidebar 7.3.

The construct being assessed is contentment with current approaches and present horizons. It centers on a personal hesitancy to become involved in anything new; it is a preference to stay with what is currently being done. The resistance is sufficient to encourage a slow response to making needed changes.

Data from the Innovation Study show that parochial schools scoring high on these items have reasons for being satisfied: teachers collaborate and work hard, students enjoy school, and parents show up for conferences. Furthermore, cost-of-living increases have been introduced for faculty; but little of an innovative nature has been introduced. Rather, a few innovations have been eliminated. Moreover, we found that these schools stayed the same over a period of three years, making no changes in how

---

SIDEBAR 7.3
Scale 12: Preference for Status Quo
(People's reaction when something new is proposed)

- I feel uneasy if a proposal seems "too new."
- I assume nothing will come of a proposed change.
- I prefer staying with what we are doing.
- I prefer to be involved only partially in new ideas.
- I feel a proposed change is being railroaded through.

they carry out their program. Obviously, their contentment with things as they are creates a resistance to anything that may change the status quo.

Ronald Lippitt, formerly a professor at the University of Michigan, views these sources of resistance in a positive way. In a speech he gave on "Utilizing Resistance as a Constructive Resource for Change," he said: "The evidence is that such resistances are not only normal, but they represent one of the best resources to help us avoid boners and locate bugs. In fact, much of the best creativity for implementing change is in the heads and experience of these question-asking 'resistors.'"[5] Lippitt goes on to say that the way to utilize this resource is to listen without defensiveness, clarify by correcting misinformation, invite people's ideas and suggestions, and then revise the first draft proposal.

According to Edward Glaser, a pioneer consultant in the field of innovation and change, "Many find it hard to believe that a frank facing of disagreements and obstacles may win more converts than an eloquent exhortation favoring their proposal."[6]

In general, a task force needs to emphasize the positive aspects of an innovation: how its results will contribute to the mission of the congregation and how the proposed change will enhance current beliefs, values, and practices.

INVOLVING LEGITIMIZERS

The involvement of legitimizers is a first and essential step in coping with resistance and gaining support for a proposed innovation. A good generalization is this: Success is positively related to the extent a task force works through opinion leaders. The questions they raise will usually anticipate the unspoken questions of resistors. The counsel they give will help sharpen the proposal and give it a greater likelihood of succeeding. And the support given by them, once they feel a psychological ownership in the project, largely assures adoption of the innovation.

You as pastor or leader of a congregation know best the approval channels a new project needs to pass through before actual adoption of an innovation is secured. And you know best which opinion makers can give legitimizing support to a new idea. Hence, your role is to guide the task force in determining which official groups and influential individuals should be involved. In general, they will consider two types of legitimizers:

the gatekeepers and the opinion makers. One type represents the formal organizational structure and the other the informal.

Gatekeepers

Every congregation has elected persons who have been charged with the responsibility of advancing the mission of some aspect of congregational life. They include the officers (president, treasurer, secretary, and the like), the boards (for example, boards of deacons, trustees, church council), and standing committees (for example, parish education, worship, music and arts, community outreach). The chairperson of each elected group may be a gatekeeper. The larger the congregation, the more gatekeepers one can expect to find.

A task force can spend a great deal of time and effort developing a plan, only to find it rejected if it fails to gain the support and commitment of the appropriate officers, board, or committee. For that reason, a task force should identify the gatekeepers whose support and active commendation is needed to give legitimacy to the planned change. Some innovations may require going through a large number of approval channels.

An unhappy experience I had in a large congregation demonstrates what can happen if a top legitimizer is not in favor of an innovation. Preliminary efforts to secure the approval and support of all legitimizers for a Vision-to-Action workshop somehow failed to gain the support of the congregation's chairman. I did not know this until the day prior to conducting the first of our two sessions.

Discovering that he was not listed as a participant, I called him. After describing what we hoped to do, and explaining that our focus was on an important part of the mission statement he and his church council had developed, I invited him to come. Discovering the first night posed a conflict, I invited him for the second night. Though he came and participated the second night, his seemingly positive evaluations of the workshop concealed his true feelings.

Later, I learned that in all subsequent council meetings (which he chaired), he prevented any of the workshop recommendations, sent first to the council, from being implemented. He successfully stymied what many had hoped would have been the beginning of a new approach to a youth and family ministry.

In a visit with gatekeepers, it is wise to do more than seek approval and support. For involvement to be truly meaningful, their counsel and advice should be sought. The questions they raise and suggestions they give will enhance the proposed innovation and, importantly, increase the likelihood of their sense of ownership.

If an innovation cuts across the domain of several boards or committees, it will be necessary to negotiate with each of these groups. Turf protection is still alive and well for most committees or boards in a church. These political realities need to be taken into consideration. Some elected persons are disturbed when they see an ad hoc group assume responsibility for an activity that falls into their assigned area.

A quick solution, of course, would be to ask the appropriate standing committee or board to assume responsibility because the proposed project relates to their designated area. Doing so, however, in most cases only sounds the death knell for the project in question. Most standing committees are not inclined to become learning groups that thoughtfully work through the steps needed to make a dream become a reality. They are not free to focus on one thing for as long as it takes that effort to be successfully launched. On the contrary, their feeling of responsibility is to maintain what has already been established.

The ideal, as indicated in chapter 3, is to use task forces or ministry teams to address emerging needs and develop innovative ministries that are responsive to current hurts and cries. Properly formed, a task force has but one concern—launching a new and desired ministry to meet the need that concerns its members.

Because most congregations have an elected committee or board system, the task force needs to negotiate a way by which it can work cooperatively with the formal structure. Its members can be asked by the appropriate committee to take the initiative for the proposed innovation, while keeping the standing committee informed and, to a degree, involved.

Opinion Makers

A less obvious but important group of people to involve are the opinion makers, who may or may not be part of the formal structure of a congregation. They are influential persons whose opinion is respected. These influential persons can promote new ideas, or they can head an active opposition. It is fair to say the success of a task force is positively related to the extent its members work through such opinion leaders. Opinion makers are ideal advocates for efforts a task force wishes to see introduced in the congregation.

A considerable number of studies on opinion makers have been carried out in various cultures. According to Everett Rogers, professor of communication research at Stanford University, who has reviewed the extensive literature on the subject, opinion makers tend to be innovative themselves and therefore are more open to proposed innovations.[7]

One of the most striking characteristics of opinion leaders is their unique and influential position in their system's communication structure: they are at the center of interpersonal communication networks. What these persons say or do tends to be heard and eventually adopted by other members of the system. Hence, they are most influential in helping to introduce needed changes.

These people are best approached informally—over a cup of coffee, at a noon luncheon, or at a gathering in one's home. During such face-to-face contacts, one can identify the need being addressed and how the innovation is focused on the congregation's mission. This is a time to welcome the opinion makers' suggestions, especially those related to values promoted in the congregation. It is a time to address the question: "How can the innovation best succeed and become a lasting, high quality contribution to the church's ministry?" Another value to consider in the discussion is the opinion makers' desire to see tangible results, such as lives being changed. Suggestions given by the opinion maker at this juncture have the likelihood of furthering the project's success.

Although involving gatekeepers and opinion makers is time consuming, the support gained saves time in the long run. It actually enhances the readiness of one's congregation to respond to other needs.[8]

An illustration of the importance of an early involvement of legitimizers, relates to the launching of the study "Early Adolescents and Their Parents" by Search Institute. Leaders in fifteen denominations and youth-serving organizations had sent letters declaring their interest in a national study focused on early adolescents and their parents. When discussing the possibilities of such a study with Robert Lynn of the Lilly Endowment, he raised this question: "Are the top persons of these groups concerned enough about their youth to support such a study and do something about the survey results?" I suggested we find out.

I traveled to each national headquarters for a two-hour session with the president of each denomination or youth serving-organization and with those people who report to this head person. Using visual aids and a series of authoritative quotes, I showed the need for the study. I presented its possible outcomes and invited their comments. Having done so, I then asked them to declare what they would be willing to do.

The outcome was beyond our fondest hopes. We received letters of strong commitment: (1) to support the three-year study; (2) to appoint a task force to begin planning for utilization efforts in years four and five, when the study would be completed; and (3) if necessary, to seek funding for program activities the study showed might be needed. One executive, following our session, had this to say: "We can participate wholeheartedly in this study because we feel we have helped launch it—it is ours." The positive attitudes of these executives established a frame of reference for the study that encouraged wide use of its outcomes.

THE TASK FORCE'S EMPHASIS

The all-important question in the minds of the legitimizers is this: "What does the task force want supported and encouraged?" Most legitimizers will be persuaded to support an effort presented to them in terms of:

- the vision the congregation wants to see implemented in the future
- the need being addressed and the expected outcome
- the innovations needed to achieve that outcome

Having identified a pressing need, the task force explains what they hope will change as a result of their vision and how they hope to bring this change about.

In the course of the conversation, the task force will describe the innovations they feel need to be introduced. An innovation may be an event, procedure, program, or new service. Each, however, is a major step being taken toward the desired outcome. If three or more innovations are mentioned, the first should be the one that requires the least amount of work and time, resulting in visible, immediate progress that all can see. The others can be sequential, moving all concerned toward the desired end.

In the course of their conversation with legitimizers, the task force will tell how they plan to work and stay with the project until their vision becomes a reality for the congregation. It is their follow-through that determines whether or not an innovation is established. Commonly, good ideas "die a borning" because there was no one person or group fighting to see the idea come alive and grow to completion.

A task force can expect leaders in a congregation to think realistically about the pros and cons of what has been presented. The obstacles they identify may well resemble the ones that surfaced in one of our research projects.[9] It is good if these obstacles can be anticipated and addressed.

SENIOR PASTOR AS KEY PERSON

The task force should know that the warm and legitimizing support of the senior pastor is of primary importance in the launching of any new idea or program. If the pastor speaks a word against a new project or simply withholds words of encouragement, the lack of interest will be noticed and resistance to the project is assured. Therefore, a task force does well to first seek the pastor's evaluation of the project. If the pastor's evaluation is encouraging, then the task force can request counsel about which gatekeepers and opinion makers should be approached. Throughout the months and possibly years of the task force's activities, the pastor should be kept informed. An important rule is to make sure there are no surprises for the pastor.

It is important to give information that shows how the proposed innovation will strengthen and enhance the ministry for which he or she is responsible. Cooperation is likely to be forthcoming when this leader sees how the proposed innovation could advance the mission of the congregation.

The importance of showing how an innovation can help the pastor surfaced in one of our research projects. It had to do with the chief executives of twenty-one agencies who refused every standardized invitation to participate in a field experiment of Search Institute. Our invitations to them included luncheons, personalized letters, telephone calls, and offers of a personal visit. The stonewalling by these executives lead us to assume, wrongly, we discovered, that they and their organizations were classic "resistors" of anything innovative.

A year and a half later, we returned to these assumed hard-core "resistors" with a simple device for gaining access to them. We approached them through a mutual friend or colleague, a friend who also knew about our project. Once in conversation with these executives, we showed them a profile printout of information that could be made available to help them understand their organization. Immediately, these administrators were interested. Here was objective data in graphic form that would identify the factors within their organization that serve to either facilitate or hinder organizational changes.

On seeing the profile printout and recognizing how such information would help them as administrators, eighteen of the twenty-one executives agreed to join the field experiment. The experience showed that these executives were not resistor types but people intent on doing their work. If information from the outside could show how something added to their program would enhance their work, then they were likely to be interested.[10]

The same observation applies also for pastors, most of whom are usually overwhelmed by many obligations. If they are shown how a proposed innovation will bless what they are seeking to do, even pastors often labeled as "resistors," are likely to become warm advocates of the task force's dream. (Chapter note 10 gives a follow-up on the "resistors.")

TENSION WITHIN THE CONGREGATION

A task force should be aware of one major roadblock members could face. It is internal tension or division within a congregation that sometimes involves the pastor. It stands in marked contrast to the three forms of resistance mentioned earlier. These first three forms can create a mild resistance within a congregation. The fourth, Internal Tension, qualifies as "divisive." If strong, it erodes group morale and siphons off desire to move ahead. It devastates an innovative atmosphere, team spirit, and feelings of organizational pride. It tends to immobilize a congregation and reduce activity to maintenance level only.

It is interesting that such tension was a threat in the congregations the apostle Paul had established. When writing to the church in Corinth, Paul ends his second letter with the words, "When I come I may not find you as I want you to be. . . . I fear that there may be quarreling, jealousy, outbursts of anger, factions, slander, gossip, arrogance and disorder" (2 Corinthians 12: 20).

Internal tension does not go unnoticed by people in a congregation. We found that of the twenty constructs measured by our instrument, none was as accurately observed by members of an organization as this one. The internal consistency of people's response to these items (see sidebar 7.4) is highest for these items.

Internal tension of the kind reflected in these items has a pervasive influence. It attacks efforts to recruit and train new people, reduces interest in evaluating what has been done, dulls interest in serving the larger community, erodes the feeling of being part of a larger mission, adds a joylessness to tasks that must be done, and creates dissatisfaction with the status quo.[11] When such tension is present a task force must expect it will take longer to win support. Greater care must be exercised in getting all opinion leaders on board and gaining the support of all members who will be affected by the innovation. This is vital if the adoption is to be a lasting one.

My associate Shelby Andress and I conducted Vision-to-Action workshops with several groups that registered high on Internal Tension. One of these groups was a college where many of the faculty and staff sharply disagreed with the leadership style of their

---

SIDEBAR 7.4
Scale 13: Internal Tension
(People become conflict weary)

- Considerable tension exists between our staff and volunteers.
- Power struggles hinder our work.
- Conflicts over values hinder our work.
- Communication is mostly one way—from the top down.
- Too much time and energy is spent in getting things approved.
- I am not happy with the way things are going in my congregation.
- Most people seem unclear about the goals of our congregation.

president. They felt communication was only a one-way street and that procedures were creating tension among faculty and staff.

The president, seeing this information in advance, was not adverse to letting it be part of the information shared at the workshop. It became part of a session where people identified what pleased or troubled them at the college. An open discussion of ways tension could be relieved proved to be helpful. The following Monday the president announced a brown bag lunch meeting with faculty to begin regularly sharing information regarding the college. Other practices that had been suggested at the workshop were adopted. A later evaluation of the president showed that many of the causes of internal tension were eliminated.

Admittedly, there is a level of conflict within a congregation that requires an outside mediator. But we found that lower levels of conflict can be reduced by frankly facing troubling issues. We found also that there is a defusing effect in the procedures of the FUTURES model:

• seeking the counsel of gatekeepers and opinion makers
• showing how an innovation can advance the mission of the congregation
• involving the opinions of all who might be impacted by the innovation
• inviting people to evaluate the innovation
• responding to people's suggestions regarding how an innovation can be improved

These procedures tend to defuse resistance by inviting broad involvement and by focusing people on the positive aspects of ministry. A task force can proceed even in the face of internal tension, because the procedures allow for facing issues and focusing on meeting a specific need.

Once legitimizers give their suggestions and support, attention can shift to the next step: rallying broad ownership for the innovation. This is done by enlisting the support of all constituent groups whose participation is desired, the subject to be discussed in the next chapter.

Reflection:
On Involving Legitimizers

• Which legitimizers in our congregation are best able to help overcome resistance to a new idea?

• What is the best way of involving our gatekeepers and opinion makers in new proposals?

• How may I as pastor breath life into our committees while giving them free reign?

• Which procedures in the FUTURES model show promise for dealing with inevitable conflicts in our congregation?

CHAPTER EIGHT

RALLY BROAD OWNERSHIP

"Involve those who have a stake in the outcome of the plan, who are impacted by the plan, and who will be asked to implement the plan."

—*Edward Glaser*

IN *MOMENTS OF TRUTH*, Jan Carlzon, president and CEO of Scandinavian Air Lines, tells how involvement of the 20,000 employees of Scandinavian Air Lines (SAS) turned the company around from financial loss to one of profitability. When he took over responsibility as CEO, he instituted a turn-around strategy of total involvement. Every employee got the same information about the company's vision and goals. Their good sense and experience was probed for ideas on how the company could improve its service to customers. Special training was given on providing service, training that meant the company was investing time and resources in their people.

The result was a change in employee attitudes, coupled with an enthusiastic feeling of responsibility to help achieve the same goal. In a single year, says Carlzon, "We had transformed a troubled airline with a morale problem, a slipping market share, and lots of red ink into exactly what we said we would become: the world's best airline for business travelers."

The employees were not forgotten when it came time to say thank you. In December every one of the twenty thousand employees received a parcel in the mail containing a beautiful gold wristwatch, a memo outlining more free trips for employees, plus a personal letter on quality parchment paper from Jan Carlzon.[1] His letter thanked them for the great job they had done in vaulting SAS from its worst loss ever to the biggest profit in its history.

This process of a broad involvement of people applies also to congregations. Where emphasized, it results in more enthusiastic support by members, a greater sense of ownership, and less resistance to something new.

BASIC STEPS IN INVOLVEMENT

Meaningful involvement includes all members who in some way will be impacted by a proposed innovation. These people need to have a part in the final shaping of the innovation, to have the sense of having contributed in some way to its development. True involvement leads to a sense of ownership in which each person feels motivated to support and further the success of the new ministry.

1. Identify Constituencies

The first step for a task force is to identify the constituencies who have a stake in the outcome, who will be impacted by the plan, and who will be asked to participate. "Innovation is facilitated by the meaningful and early involvement of those who will implement change, and it is seriously hampered when participants are not involved."[2]

Let's suppose a proposed innovation seeks to introduce a new youth program, such as peer ministry. A basic step will be to involve the youth by first discussing the idea with some of youth's opinion leaders. They can help by anticipating the reaction of other youth and by suggesting how best to introduce the program to the entire youth group.

Some innovations require the involvement of several constituency groups. Let's suppose the vision championed by the task force is to develop a contemporary Sunday service that is inspirational and meaningful for both unchurched outsiders and current members. This objective impacts many groups, not least the old-timers, for whom traditional services have been meaningful for many years.

It is important that a task force gain the counsel of these old-timers as well as those representing a variety of cultures. The question to be raised is, "What in a worship service inspires you, is especially meaningful to you, and helps you commune with God?" The people quizzed should range from members raised on liturgical services to outsiders, who are often puzzled by church symbols and turned off by eighteenth- and nineteenth-century hymns. Uppermost in these conversations, however, must be a congregation's need to reach the many outsiders for whom a traditional worship service may be unattractive.

Following their interviews, the task force might visit other congregations that have developed contemporary worship services. Practices that seem to fit their congregation might then be introduced on a trial basis. People's evaluation of what is introduced can be determined initially from their comments and by the way they vote with their feet.

Once the congregation has experienced the innovation for a time, the task force might prepare an evaluation survey containing items that identify the full range of people's opinions. This survey instrument ideally should be given to a random sample of people. If necessary, a follow-up contact should be made to ensure that responses are obtained from a majority of the sample. Respondents should be asked to indicate their age, frequency of worship attendance, and the number of years they have attended a worship service. The report should use these three variables to classify people's responses.

An alternative to a survey would be to hold focus groups. Group members should be chosen to represent the different populations being served by the congregation. People in these groups could be asked questions similar to those included in the survey. One advantage of focus groups is that you can ask questions about people's reasons for their response.

David S. Luecke, in *The Other Story of Lutherans at Worship*,[3] gives a history of the rapid growth in congregations that have introduced contemporary worship services. He notes that five features characterize these services.

1. They feature music that tends to have emotionally expressive melodies amply supported by instruments.

2. Services are typically visitor friendly, made simple and easy to follow.

3. Informality is emphasized for the sake of good communication, a key objective in a contemporary service.

4. Services feature revitalized preaching where a text is unfolded into application or where the sermon starts with the needs of listeners.

5. Services involve many people in the service as lay readers, singers and musicians, speakers, and persons who share their personal faith.

Billy Graham, wanting to reach young people through his evangelistic crusades, noted that young people are less attracted to the singing of Beverly Shea or church choirs. Therefore, he introduced the music of a Christian rock group at his crusade in Cleveland in 1994. Though most adults would not know the group called D.C. Talk or appreciate their music, this rock group and its style of music represents today's youth's culture.

The appeal of D.C. Talk was evident in the fact that over sixty-five thousand people, mostly youth, came to the Saturday youth night service in Minneapolis in June 1996. Evidence that the group's singing communicated the gospel and provided a good preparation for Graham's message was seen in an unprecedented response to Graham's invitation at the end of the service. There were not enough counselors to care for the many youth who wanted to commit their lives to Christ. A clearly defined target group was reached through music that is part of their world.

2. Involve Constituencies

A second meaningful step in involving people is to identify the need being addressed and show how a proposed innovation might advance the congregation's mission. This step may be no more than meeting with the youth group to alert them to the need for peer counseling among young people they know. All of them have had experiences of providing a shoulder for some one to cry on. What is their reaction to a program that would equip them to be a friend to a peer in time of trouble? The innovation they might consider is a peer ministry training program that has revolutionized congregational youth groups elsewhere.

Once conversation has started, the task force can present its vision along with a tentative plan for bringing reality to the vision. The plan should be presented as a tentative one, because the task force hopes to hear suggestions that will improve the proposal. They also hope to hear suggestions about how these participants may help.

Involvement, however, can be sought for an innovation far larger than a program. The innovation may potentially affect not just one constituency group but an entire congregation. A classic example is found in the need being faced by Our Saviour's Lutheran Church, whose beautiful building, stained glass windows, and new pipe organ all went up in flames one Friday night in Minneapolis, shortly before Christmas 1995.

This historic congregation, begun in 1869, grew to 1,600 members under the leadership of a distinguished roster of pastors. Known as a missionary church, it has a history of establishing innovative ministries as well as eight new congregations in the city of Minneapolis.

But as its inner-city neighborhood declined, members began moving out to the suburbs. Though membership loss was persistent, a core group remained, convinced that God's mission for them was to be Christ's presence in their area, known as the Phillips neighborhood. This neighborhood, with a medium income of $7,000 a year, has among its many minority populations, six thousand Native Americans, the largest number found in any city in the United States. Unfortunately, it has earned the reputation of being a high-crime area.

In this setting, before the fire, Our Saviour's 250 active members had developed an amazing ministry. The congregation provided housing in their church gymnasium for forty homeless men each night and transitional housing for several families. It established an English Learning Center for refugees and immigrants, where as many as 125 people attended classes four evenings a week to learn English and the use of computers. In one year, 600 people were taught by tutors, volunteers who in turn are trained by the Minnesota Literary Council.

In addition, the congregation had a children's after-school program. During school vacation days, the program was run all day. When summer arrived, children were provided activities for eight weeks to help parents unable to care for their children during the day because of work. Needless to say, this ministry by 250 members and several hundred volunteers was using every space in the church building seven days a week. All this was in addition to the regular church program of Bible studies, Sunday school, choir, youth program, and so forth.

Then came the fire that destroyed all the facilities. In the year that followed, the church council, serving like a task force in a larger congregation, involved members through retreats and workshops in shaping a new vision of their future. Determined to stay in the area, the questions were these: What does God have in mind for us? What should be our ministry in the future? What partnerships might we establish with other congregations, social service agencies, schools, and community organizations?

Providentially, insurance on the destroyed church provided a legacy of $3.4 million that began drawing interest while a new vision was being shaped by members. Before rebuilding, they wanted to know what the new structure must accommodate. As stated by a council member, "When the walls came down for this congregation, all that was left were horizons on all sides." Members enlarged their vision during these times of involvement. And interestingly, the growing sense of excitement caused their membership to increase.[4]

Constituency involvement is widely recognized as important because members and stakeholders within organizations are becoming increasingly diverse. It is commonly understood that a shared purpose cannot be imposed on a constituency by its leaders or a task force. Members want to participate in some meaningful way through a process of collaboration.

Peter Senge underscores this idea: "The origin of a vision (whether from an individual or top down) is much less important than the process whereby it comes to be shared. It is truly not a shared vision until it connects with the personal visions of people throughout the organization." That is why, before an innovation is launched, the vision needs to be discussed with the groups impacted by the innovation and their suggestions need to be welcomed.

Senge adds, "In a corporation, a shared vision changes people's relationship with the company. It is no longer 'their company'; it becomes 'our company.' A shared vision is the first step in allowing people who mistrusted each other to begin to work together. It creates a common identity."[5]

Each time the task force presents its vision to a different constituency, the vision spreads and with it promotes increasing clarity, enthusiasm, and commitment. As people talk, the vision grows clearer. As it gets clearer, enthusiasm for its benefits builds.

Meaningful involvement results in members of a constituency becoming aware of the need being addressed, excited about possibilities in the proposed vision, and able to see how they can help bring it about. Meaningful involvement also means being kept informed about progress and appraised when the first innovation is introduced.

I was present one Wednesday evening when members of an inner-city church came together to discuss how best to inaugurate several additions to their current ministry. In a Vision-to-Action workshop they had envisioned their church becoming a resource for family problems and issues, a place for intergenerational faith sharing, a spiritual center for people in the community, a place where ethnic diversity is welcomed with a ministry that enhances parent-youth communication. As a result of this meeting, plans were made to involve the entire membership in launching a multiphase program on Wednesday nights. The program was also designed to involve people in the immediate community.

MODELING AND TEACHING INVOLVEMENT

The procedures used by a task force to involve people do more than help launch an innovation. They also teach constituent groups a cycle of involvement: how to focus on a need, evaluate need in light of the church's mission, formulate a vision that does something about the need, and share the vision with others. A task force can demonstrate how to listen to people, do need-focused planning, communicate plans, and follow through when launching a new ministry.

When repeated over time by various task forces, these procedures help the congregation develop the skill to proceed when suddenly faced with a desperate need. When regularly practiced, the procedures will enhance the likelihood of a congregation developing a readiness to act.

Of the various learned procedures, two that are extremely useful for people in a congregation are listening to needs and communicating with constituencies. Where these were especially emphasized by congregations, agencies, or schools in the Innovation Study, the following characteristics were consistently identified: (1) groups were able to sustain worthwhile changes introduced in previous years, and (2) the groups introduced few but lasting innovations.

Listening to Needs

Listening surfaces problems and stimulates conversations on possible solutions. It enables a task force to learn from constituent groups in the church and helps establish a feeling of mutuality— the sense that what is being done, is done by all of us. This is a characteristic highly valued in a pastor. Note sidebar 8.1.

The effects of such a listening stance were clearly evident in congregations of the Innovation Study where this was stressed. Among the parochial schools that scored high on this scale:

- new activities were introduced which served the larger community
- a shift took place in religious emphasis, a greater balance was established between the experiential and cognitive in religion courses
- freshman programs that aid in study skills and personal adjustment were added

Significantly, the three judges rated these groups high on innovativeness and openness to new ideas.[6]

SIDEBAR 8.1
Scale 14: Listening to Needs
(People listen to others' needs)

- We take time to hear what people feel is needed before introducing changes.
- We stimulate an awareness of the urgent needs of the people we serve.
- We seek the reaction of people we serve to a proposed program.
- We evaluate our progress toward clearly defined goals.
- We hear enthusiastic comments about our programs from people we serve.

Communicating with Constituencies

The second important element in involvement is staying in touch with constituencies regarding what is proposed. We were impressed with the sensitivity that innovative groups showed with respect to keeping in touch with their people. Granted, much of the communicating did occur informally. When task force members are enthusiastic about their congregation and its work, they find it natural to communicate what is happening with appropriate constituencies. Informally, they tend to talk about their plans and speak about what they see happening in the future. It should come as no surprise to learn that there is a high correlation between the items noted in sidebar 8.2 and the scale mentioned earlier, Organizational Pride.

From these items one can infer that the underlying construct is maintaining contact with constituencies. In the Innovation Study, 4-H groups that stressed this made special efforts to hear how the community felt about their programs and staff activities. Also observed were efforts to gain a greater understanding of the interests, concerns, and goals of their members.

When adult leaders of church youth groups emphasized maintaining contact with their people, the following characteristics appeared.

- parents felt informed
- intergenerational meetings were held
- volunteer leaders were attracted to the group
- more leaders attended training workshops

SIDEBAR 8.2
Scale 15: Communicating with Constituencies
(People are kept informed)

- There is enthusiastic, informal sharing of ideas among members of our group.
- We discuss the best time to introduce a new program.
- We try to inform those we serve about why we do what we do.
- We share information on innovations well in advance of a decision to adopt them.

Apparently, regularly giving information about one's program stimulates both people's interest in the activities and their willingness to support what is being done. Maintaining contact with constituencies through various kinds of communication is an important accent in any aspect of a congregation's life.

As each task force learns to listen to needs and to communicate with constituencies, they are both modeling and teaching how a congregation can become more innovative and responsive. The innovations they launch using these procedures are likely to become lasting ones, with the added bonus of seeing positive attitudes develop among members and staff toward making changes. When members of a task force function as a learning or ministry team, they are learning to become lay leaders in the congregation.

THE PHENOMENON OF INVOLVEMENT

Involvement of people is a value orientation that finds its expression on several levels that vary from nominal participation to deep commitment. No matter what the level, however, the effects of involvement are impressive. Consider its power even when the motivation for involvement is no more than to increase the number of people who participate. That describes the nature of the items used in the Innovation Study. In spite of this low level of motivation, groups placing a high value on choosing programs simply to involve more people, also show up as being more innovative. Notice in the items of sidebar 8.3 the considerations deemed important when evaluating the worth of a new program.

Organizations favoring programs simply because they will involve more people and increase membership still experience

---

SIDEBAR 8.3
Scale 16: Involvement of People
(People are encouraged to participate)

- A new program will help us get more people involved.
- A new program will help expand our membership.
- More than one age group will be involved in launching a new program together.
- People say they like the new program.

---

higher morale and more enthusiastic support from their constituencies.[7] But most congregations wish to involve people for
more reasons than to swell the membership and see larger
turnouts.

Involvement Leads to Commitment

There is a higher level of involvement that brings people past
compliance to a deep sense of commitment, the kind of involvement sought by most organizations. In the words of Peter Senge,
"Few subjects are closer to the hearts of contemporary managers
than commitment." He goes on, "The word 'committed' describes
a state of not only being enrolled (becoming part of something
by choice), but feeling fully responsible for making the vision
happen."[8]

If a minimal level of involvement can energize a group to excel
in innovative actions, consider the result when members of a congregation are fully committed to bringing a much desired vision.
Committed persons bring an energy, passion, and excitement that
goes well beyond being involved in a casual way. A group of people truly committed to a common vision can be an awesome force.

Congregations valuing the involvement of people for more reasons than increasing membership, approach governance with the
conviction that God's Spirit speaks through his people. In such
churches, the membership is involved in solving problems, making decisions, and implementing those decisions. With this level
of involvement comes a higher degree of member responsibility
and a wider acceptance of parish objectives.

Where this approach to governance is not valued, the tendency
is to restrict decision making to a few, to control what is said, and
to let the pastor determine what is to be done. When the work is
being done by a few, the pastor usually experiences overload.

Paul Stevens, author of Liberating the Laity, in the "Laity
Exchange" newsletter establishes the premise upon which involvement of members in a congregation should take place. He writes:

> Laity is a word derived from the Greek word for "people" and
> it means all the people of God (1 Peter 2.9-10). It is a term of
> incredible honor. In Christ all the laity become ministering
> persons. They are not merely the recipients of ministry from
> pastors, missionaries, and theologians. The laity ARE the

ministers. They are the means by which Jesus continues to minister in the world in the power of His Spirit. And the job of pastors is not to do the ministry themselves, but "to equip all the saints for the work of ministry" (Ephesians 4: 11-12 RSV).[9]

Paul Powell, in *The Nuts and Bolts of Church Growth*, also stresses this point:

> The first responsibility of the pastor is to prepare people to minister for Christ. Even if the pastor can do it all in some church settings, this is not the pastor's proper role. The laity must be trained to be the ministers, and opportunities for ministry must be created by them and for them.[10]

One can argue that involvement should be seen as going beyond church activities to include all aspects of life—one's work as a homemaker or teacher or factory worker. Quaker educator and philosopher Elton Trueblood underscores this point when saying, "Church-goer is a vulgar, ignorant word and should never be used. You cannot go to church, you are the church wherever you go."[11]

In *Prepare Your Church for the Future*, Carl George recommends a higher level of member involvement than has characterized churches in the past. It is a new paradigm, which he has labeled meta-church. It is an approach to involvement in which all members are organized in home-cell units of ten for the purpose of Bible study, spiritual nurture, outreach, and service. By organizing a congregation's caring and leadership formation around this building block of a ten-person cell, a church of any size can ensure high quality care at a very intense level.[12]

This meta-church principle originated with Pastor David Yonggi Cho, of the Yoido Central Full Gospel Church in Seoul, Korea, a congregation of 650,000 parishioners who regularly participate in home groups for Bible study and prayer. He established the cell of ten people with a leader and understudy as the foundational unit of his congregation. The leader functions as a lay pastor to this ten-person flock. The purpose of each group is for members to nurture and care for one another and to use their gifts for a "one another" ministry. It is expected that each cell will expand as nonmembers are invited to join them. Once it has over twelve members, the cell subdivides, with leadership of the new cell being taken over by the leader in training. Birthing of a new cell can be motivated also by tension or discontent.

An important feature is the training of cell leaders. They, with their understudy, meet regularly to report; to identify problems; and to plan, share, and learn from one another. These are times when the coach, either a pastor or staff member, helps these lay ministers with encouragement and guidance in leading groups.

A striking illustration of the effectiveness of this total involvement of members is given by Pastor Dale Galloway, founding pastor of New Hope Community Church, Portland, Oregon. While at home, he received a telephone call summoning him to a home in his community. A grisly and bizarre murder had taken place in a distant state involving as a suspect the alienated foster child of one of the families in his church. He decided to go immediately to give his moral support to the family.

Upon arriving, he saw the local news teams already filming the house from the street. But arriving at the door he saw one of the members of the family's cell group (called TLC, Tender, Loving Care) guarding the door and detaining journalists. Once inside, he saw another member of the TLC group lining up meals for the family and screening incoming calls. In the living room he saw a third member of the TLC group comforting the family.

All there was for Pastor Dale Galloway to do was give the grieving family a hug, lead in prayer, and ask what else he could do. He was told, "Everything is under control. It was nice of you to come by."

Here is an illustration of a congregation where members have been equipped with a readiness to act, to respond quickly to unexpected needs and situations. Their involvement in small caring groups had prepared them for innovative acts of service and love. They had learned from one another how to live out the mission of Jesus Christ.

The Community and Public Image

Another form of involvement relates to the larger community of which the church is a part. In the Innovation Study we found two contrasting motives for seeking a favorable public image. One motive, seemingly, was to gain a favorable public impression, which differs from what exists in reality. The other motive was to share enthusiasm and joy over good things that are happening in the hope that outsiders might be attracted to one's church or school.

The negative motive became evident in the following way. We found the least innovative and progressive schools in one of our sample groups placing a highest value on good public relations. As a result, an unprecedented fifteen criterion items (descriptions of innovative activities) correlated negatively with this measure. The only conclusion we could draw is that these noninnovative and unprogressive schools (as judged by the three people who observed them over a three-year period) were conscious of being viewed unfavorably. Hence, they placed a stronger value on the items listed in sidebar 8.4 because they hoped to change the image they knew many held of their schools. They wanted to be seen in a favorable light, even if it meant being seen as different from what was true of their group.

A positive motive seems to have been operating for the adult leaders of congregational youth groups in the United Methodist and Lutheran congregations. Their underlying desire when answering these items was to let others know some of the good things being done by their youth groups. In congregations where adult leaders placed a high value on these items, the youth groups tended to be innovative (again as judged by the three observers). Here are descriptions of two innovative activities characterizing these congregations, ones the adult leaders might have wanted people in the community to know about:

• A group has formed to carry out a service project related to environmental concerns (for example, recycling waste, city clean-up).

• Parents have rallied to support the youth groups (for example, fund raising, advisory groups, public relations).

SIDEBAR 8.4
Scale 17: Favorable Public Image
(People are intent on a good public image)

- I believe the proposed activity will make our local organization look good.
- I believe the activity will benefit me.
- The proposed activity could draw a lot of favorable publicity.
- I had a part in shaping or evaluating the proposed activity.

Kennon Callahan speaks about the importance of a favorable public image, which is gained in two principle ways. One is the visibility gained when the pastor and key leaders in the church participate in a broad range of community activities in the area served by the church. This, which is appreciated, reflects well on the church.

The other is the favorable public image gained through the informal network of relationships in a community. Enthusiastic comments of members, delighted with what God is doing and accomplishing in the lives of people, travels fast over the informal network. Barna speaks of this as a selfless pride: "People are excited to belong to a community of believers who have done a mighty work. They are proud to be a part of a world in which their lives make a difference."[13] Such people place a high value on letting others know about what is happening.

According to Lyle Schaller, people in a community have a definite image of growing churches that is based on what they do best. Hence, people will say, "That's the church with a good youth program" or "They have the best music in town."[14] Kennon Callahan echoes this point of view: "A church that has successfully developed a major program that meets community's standards in that specific field of endeavor earns community-wide respect for that program." He notes also that "churches with a good public image are those with a reputation of being a source of help, reliability, and certainty for people struggling with the difficulties and transitions of every day life."[15]

Members who place a high value on letting others know about the good things happening in their congregation serve as a force within a congregation. By sharing what is happening as their congregational vision unfolds, they encourage others to be a part of the innovative and progressive activities within the congregation.

Admittedly, our measure of the value people place on a favorable public image is a most limited one. It focuses on the minimal or most superficial aspects of this value. Nevertheless, even at this level, the desire for a favorable image is still a significant force within an organization. How much more, then, will this value be a force within a congregation when the viewpoint is that of the apostle Peter: "Live such good lives among the pagans that, though they accuse you of doing wrong, they may see your good deeds and glorify God on the day he visits us" (1 Peter 2:12). Or that of unbelievers, who observed of the Christians of their day: "Behold, how they love one another."

Reflection:
How We Rally Ownership

• How might we involve our members to increase their sense of ownership in a project before it is launched?

• How well do we listen to our constituency groups and share our plans for meeting needs they identify?

• How might we apply the meta-church approach, so every member is involved in some form of ministry?

• What image do people in the community have of our congregation?

CHAPTER NINE

ENGAGE IN ACTION

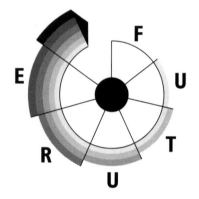

"Creativity is thinking up new things. Innovation is doing new things."

— *Theodore Leavitt*

THE TASK OF IMPLEMENTATION

GREAT IDEAS NEED TO BE IMPLEMENTED. To ensure that action takes place and something significant happens, the task of innovation should not be taken from the initiating team or task force and turned over to another group. Especially avoid turning the task over to a standing committee whose area of responsibility happens to include the innovation.

I served as chairman of a task force intent on establishing a youth and family ministry in our congregation. We interviewed every family in our congregation regarding the kinds of ministries they would appreciate. Our task force discussed their suggestions and concerns and planned to respond to them. But when a standing committee whose responsibilities overlapped with what we hoped to establish heard of our plans, they made comments that smacked of turf protection.

Glad to turn implementation over to an appropriate committee, I met with those who were present at their monthly meeting, hoping to bring them on board and to see them take responsibility for the innovation. Because only half of the committee members were present, they asked if I could meet with them next month when the rest could hear what we were proposing. The other half were present that month but not the first group. Even with this group, there was very little time for my presentation because they had other items on their agenda.

The upshot of my efforts was a clear awareness that implementation of a dream or vision cannot be turned over to another group, even though the committee structure seems to require it. A committee that has no ownership of an idea, no background or special feeling for what is proposed, will not be able to establish a lasting innovation. The task force nurturing the idea should be given the authorization and support to take whatever time is required to bring the vision into reality. The task of implementation requires both a strategy and careful preparation. Slighting these two important considerations will result in promising innovations being dropped or launched in ways that cannot succeed.

INTRODUCING AN INNOVATION

Robert W. Ackerman, a business consultant in corporate planning, had some good words of advice on launching an innovation. He stresses taking slow or partial steps that do not risk the entire project. He advocates sending out test balloons and watching for emerging trends or tendencies. Then he encourages people to air their concerns and frustrations with the unknown, and finally to allow time for clarifying existing questions.[1]

Trial on a Partial Basis

One useful strategy is to try out an innovation on a small scale or temporary basis. When people know it is temporary and for the purpose of evaluation, they are far more likely to withhold judgment and to cooperate with what is being tried.

Jack Rothman, a research psychologist, became convinced of this through his studies on research utilization. "Innovations amenable to trial on a partial basis will have a higher adoption rate than innovations necessitating total adoption without an anticipatory trial." The evidence is strong that doing part of an innovation enhances the likelihood that it will be adopted when finally introduced on a full-scale basis.

In light of this fact, a task force should introduce their innovation as a trial that later will be evaluated. If this approach is used members can expect the least resistance and the most support from people in the congregation. By way of contrast, introducing an innovation on a large scale with the intent of trying to involve everyone will be difficult to do and sustain.

An illustration of how introducing an innovation on a trial basis can further the adoption of an innovation is found in the Readiness for Ministry Project sponsored by the Association of Theological Schools in North America and Canada. The innovation was an instrument that assessed the readiness of seminarians for ministry. It had been developed by Search Institute using data from a comprehensive survey of pastors, laity, and seminarians randomly selected from within the forty-seven denominations whose seminaries are accredited by the Association of Theological Schools.

The instrument, developed through procedures common to the social sciences, was seen as an intrusion by many faculty whose theological and philosophical orientation was anti-social science. Their natural stance was to resist the use of such an assessment. Yet they recognized that a carefully developed instrument could serve an important purpose in evaluating a seminarian's fitness to take on a parish ministry, an issue for many people.

Rather than require seminaries to adopt the instrument and use it with all seminarians, the Association of Theological Schools used this strategy. On a trial basis, it was to be given only to first-year students. The intent was to monitor these students and see whether deficits that appeared in their profile were eliminated during the seminary experience. Because the program was made voluntary by the accrediting agency and the focus was on first-year students only, most seminary faculties voted to accept the innovation on a trial basis. Later, when it became apparent that the instrument was useful in assessing readiness for ministry, most of the seminaries agreed to keep the instrument as part of their testing program.

When introducing an innovation on a trial basis, it is also good strategy to maximize the likelihood of a successful trial run. One way to ensure success is to involve potential users in the field-testing process. It gives them a sense of ownership in what is being introduced. Another tactic is to involve "early innovators" and gain their help in developing an exemplary trial run. If a trial run does not go well under more or less ideal conditions, the task force can be concerned about the viability of their proposed innovation.

Preparing for Implementation

Careful preparation, a second consideration, includes taking seriously several of the steps already described in our conceptual model:

- Uniting people by instilling a sense of the compelling need.
- Tying the proposed innovation to the congregation's mission and values.
- Using the input of legitimizers to improve what is being proposed.
- Rallying broad ownership among those most impacted by the innovation.

These important steps are basic to launching what is hoped will become a lasting innovation of quality and significance. Groups successful in introducing needed change give considerable attention to the details of careful preparation. Their commitment shows itself in a desire to make sure the programs will impact lives in a positive way. Note the kind of preparation included in this construct, outlined in sidebar 9.1.

SIDEBAR 9.1
Scale 18: Preparing Carefully for Change
(Support is gained in advance)

- We consider how to increase people's sense of need for the new program being introduced.
- We discuss the success that other congregations have had with certain programs.
- We spend the time needed to test a new program before introducing it.
- We gain the endorsement of known and respected people before launching new programs.
- We seek out new ways to do our work by reviewing what others write.

ACTION PLAN—Worksheet II

Desired Outcome:

	KEY CONSIDERATIONS	ACTION STEPS	PERSONS RESPONSIBLE	WHEN?
Legitimizers	Whose support and approval do we need?	How do we gain support?	Who does what?	By what dates?
Stakeholders	What groups need to own what we propose?	How do we involve these groups?	Who does what to involve them?	By what dates?
Need	How do we create an awareness of need for our desired outcome?	What approach should be used with each group?	Who will do what to create an awareness of need?	
Mission	Which of our values are linked to the outcome we seek?	Which values should we stress with each group?		

Task Force Members: Date:

The goal is that people's first exposure to an innovation results in the most positive response possible. Though careful preparation takes more time, it pays off in more lasting innovations. Congregations in the Innovation Study who excelled in careful planning rated high in innovativeness and in their effectiveness in gaining a broad base of support.[2]

An illustration of why careful preparation is needed for launching an innovation is found in an analysis made by the dean of American pollsters, Daniel Yankelovich. He notes that public opinion on any issue develops slowly over a long period—at least ten years for a complex issue. Furthermore, he observes that the public goes through seven stages before it is ready to act. The stages listed below may resemble what many a pastor has observed about his or her congregation.

1. Awareness: People first become aware of an issue.

2. Urgency: They develop a sense of urgency about it.

3. Exploration: They start to explore choices for dealing with the issue.

4. Resistance: Resistance to facing costs and trade-offs begins to kick in, producing wishful thinking.

5. Evaluation: People weigh the pros and cons of alternatives.

6. Decision: They take a stand intellectually.

7. Action: They make a responsible judgment morally and emotionally.[3]

It is this slow response to anything new that a task force must consider when seeking to introduce something they are convinced is needed immediately. Included in their consideration must be an awareness of how their congregation is organized. The more structured and attuned it is to correct procedure, the longer will be the time required to introduce something new.

AN IMPLEMENTATION TIMELINE

There comes a time when a task force must put wheels under its plan of action. This means deciding what steps will be required to launch the innovation on a trial run basis, who will be responsible for seeing that these steps are taken, and when each step should be taken. To help in this kind of planning, make available for each member Action Plan Worksheet II (on page 152). Note on this worksheet that the first entry is identifying the desired outcome, the focus for all the planning. It is important that the team keeps before it the vision members want to see become a reality. That is why it is helpful to write the desired outcome on the top of the planning worksheet.

Once a sketch of activities has been established, it is useful to take the time required to anticipate possible roadblocks that might be encountered in the implementation of an innovation. Laura Spencer, a business consultant with multinational corporations, in *Winning Through Participation,* refers to this effort as an exercise in naming underlying contradictions—that is, situations, both internal and external, that can get in the way to obstruct or even prevent a successful innovation.[4] A task force should expect obstacles to the adoption of an innovation to surface once a group gives it serious consideration. These obstacles need to be systematically faced before a trial takes place. Taking time to do this adds a note of realism to planning.

Shelby Andress has developed a set of questions, using our conceptual model, that help anticipate possible obstructions to an innovation. Her list of questions (see sidebar 9.2) can help your task force identify situations they ought to anticipate. Once possible roadblocks are identified, a team can brainstorm possible ways of countering the most formidable of these obstacles. The steps chosen for countering possible obstructions can be added to the plan of action.

SIDEBAR 9.2
Anticipating Obstacles

Instruction: Take three to four minutes to brainstorm responses to the following questions. Keep in mind the rules for brainstorming:

- Call out ideas quickly.
- Do not evaluate or make judgments.
- Write down every idea.

1. What possible obstacles or resistances to our innovation should we anticipate?
2. What supportive forces could help us achieve our goal?
3. What concrete actions could be taken to overcome resistance and take advantage of supportive forces?

Inasmuch as a congregational task force consists of a group of volunteers who have only a limited amount of time, it is good to assign responsibility for specific steps to teams of two persons. Thus the task can be divided so no one person is given excessive work.

Each team of two, meeting separately, can prepare an implementation brief that identifies who is responsible to do what, as well as when each of these responsibilities should be completed. Implementation briefs are written plans. One of the classic publications in the field of organizational change emphasizes the need for plans to be written down. The author insists:

> Require written work plans, outlining how the individual team intends to accomplish its goals. The plans should include specific steps in each assignment, the names of people who will be contacted, the names of those responsible for each step, and dates by which each step is to be completed.[5]

When the teams of two reassemble, the task force chair can develop a large timeline, arranged by weeks, that shows what will be done by each member during the next three to six months. As each team of two reports their intended activities, information can be written on the timeline specifying what is to be done, who is responsible, and the dates by which each activity will be completed. Seeing the sequence of tasks outlined in chart form helps a task force move energetically into the implementation stage. See Action Plan Worksheet III (on page 156).[6]

UNDERGIRDING ACTION WITH PRAYER

Planning for a successful trial of the innovation is a prelude to launching the larger effort. Though a prelude, the task is significant because it establishes how meetings are conducted. Something more profound than careful planning can occur in the lives of task force members. Hence, a discussion of a Bible passage and sharing faith stories should be a part of each meeting. Such an interchange will result in members drawing closer to each other. Thus meetings are a time for becoming both a learning team and a fellowship group.

Meetings are also times when members can draw closer to their Lord, when plans are laid before God in prayer, asking for God's guidance, blessing, and empowerment. It is at these times that

ACTION PLAN—Worksheet III

Desired Outcome:

Innovation _____ (copy)

ALREADY IN PLACE (to build on)	ACTION STEPS	WHO ARE RESPONSIBLE? Individual(s), Group(s)	WHEN? Show beginning and end of Months, Qtrs., Yrs X- - - - - - -X

Task Force Members: Date:

members reflect on the unique quality of a congregation, namely, its dialectic as both a human and a divine institution. It is vital that the task force looks to an eternal God to provide what human hands cannot accomplish.

Reflection:
On Getting Started

• Has the chair met with the committee to discuss beginning steps using Action Plan—Worksheet I?

• Do members of the committee or task force see how their desired outcome advances the mission of the congregation?

• Has there been discussion regarding the various people to involve, as called for in Worksheet II?

•Are the steps to be taken during the next weeks and months recorded on Worksheet III?

• Has the seeking of God's guidance through prayer and the discussion of scripture become part of each meeting?

CHAPTER TEN

SUSTAIN
THE INNOVATIONS
LONG-TERM

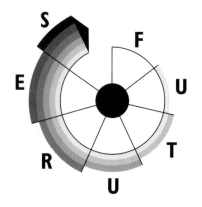

*"The 'adoption' of a rec-
ommended innovation
should not be a finished
act; it should only be the
beginning of a continu-
ing process that may lead
to something much better
than the original design."*

—*Edward Glaser*

A COMMON FALLACY is to assume that an innovation must succeed its first year. Not realizing that time is required for significant change, a task force may drop a promising program or challenging vision because initially it does not gain quick, wide acceptance. Your role as congregational leader is to encourage a long-
term approach, emphasizing that it may take several years and several innovations to achieve a desired outcome.

A long-term approach views the launching of an innovation as
a continuing process and not a finished act. The approach is characterized by a listening stance wherein members of the task force
listen for the reactions of constituency groups within the church

to see whether the innovation needs altering to gain a more positive response. This process of evaluation with subsequent revisions, is what Peters and Waterman advocate: "Do it, fix it, try it." Underlying these evaluations is the intent to determine whether the original need is being met and the mission of the congregation is being advanced.

Key to this sustained approach is the ongoing work of the task force, which needs to remain committed to its vision and persevere in its effort to establish a new form of ministry in the congregation. Establishing a new form of ministry requires thought, study, evaluation, and the seeking of God's guidance. Carried out over time, the process can become a learning experience in which members grow in their understanding of ministry and the dynamics of change. Because the success of a task force is increased by its becoming a learning team, this chapter is focused on the following four topics:

- learning to function as a team
- learning from evaluations
- learning through in-service training
- learning through God's guidance

LEARNING TO FUNCTION AS A TEAM

The task force intent on bringing into being a much desired form of ministry cannot take for granted its ability to achieve good group interaction. Members must go through a process of learning how to function as a group.

In *Organizational Culture and Leadership*, Edgar H. Schein, professor of management at Massachusetts Institute of Technology, speaks of his experience with groups that have just been formed. Initially, he says, each member is struggling with the personal issues of inclusion, identity, authority, and intimacy. The group is really not a group but a collection of individuals, each focused on how to make the situation safe and personally rewarding. In other words, at this stage people are much more preoccupied with their own feelings than with the problem of the group as a group. It is his observation that a group goes through four stages of evolution with each stage having a characteristic that is established by the dominant assumption of the group. (See sidebar 10.1.)

STAGE	CHARACTERISTIC	DOMINANT ASSUMPTION
One	Group Formation	Dependence *"The leader knows what we should do."*
Two	Group Building	Fusion *"We are a great group; we all like each other."*
Three	Group Work	Work well *"We work effectively; we know each other."*
Four	Group Maturity	Maturity *"We know who we are, what we want, and how to get it."*[1]

A task force needs to spend some time working through its natural dependence on a leader and moving on to the point where members come to like each other and feel they are a great group. This is a necessary first step if they are to function as a group to carry out a long-term approach to innovation.

Peter Senge believes team learning takes place when team members master two forms of communication: dialogue (parties gain insights that could not be achieved individually) and conversation (participants exchange thoughts and information in Ping-Pong fashion). Teams prevent productive dialogue and conversation by using "defensive routines" such as smoothing over differences when faced with conflict, or speaking out in a winner-take-all, free-for-all of opinion sharing. These defensive routines can, however, have the potential to foster learning.[2]

David Bohm, a leading quantum theorist, saw an analogy between the collective properties of particles and the way thought works. He believes we must look on thought as a systemic phenomenon arising from the way we interact and engage in discourse with others. Intent on developing a theory and method of dialogue, he presents these three basic conditions for a group to to gain a "pool of common meaning" through the use of dialogue:

1. All participants must "suspend" their assumptions, literally to hold them "as if suspended before us."

2. All participants must regard one another as colleagues.

3. There must be a facilitator who "holds the context" of the dialogue.[3]

The leadership of a facilitator is important in helping a group become a group and in learning how to carry out the kind of dialogue where members are willing to play with new ideas, to examine them, and test them out.

To help bring this about, Senge makes three suggestions for the facilitator. First, help people in the group maintain ownership of the process and the outcomes of the discussion. Second, keep the dialogue moving when individuals try to divert the process. And third, be willing to influence the dialogue by saying what needs to be said at various points.[4]

As a facilitator of groups, I have found the following two procedures useful in helping a group get started. The first procedure is to involve the group in describing the kind of interaction and commitment they want from members of their group. During our first session I list on a board, the kinds of interaction they desire for their group (for example, all participating, all free to express ideas) and the kinds of commitment they want from each other (for example, regular attendance). This list of characteristics, useful in setting an initial tone for the group, are also useful when evaluating how well the group is functioning. At various times during the year, I place their list of desired characteristics on a chalk board and ask them to evaluate the quality of their current meetings against this list.

A second procedure I have found helpful is a fun activity. I begin by introducing participants to the range of roles commonly played in groups. I hand them a sheet that includes descriptions of positive roles (for example, encourager, harmonizer, initiator, opinion seeker, summarizer) and negative roles (for example, dominator, blocker, aggressor, cry baby, antagonizer). (Descriptions of these roles are found in Appendix B.)

At a subsequent session I hand out slips of paper describing two negative roles for each person to play in the course of our conversation. It is not long after introducing a topic for discussion that conversation grinds to a halt. All see vividly the effects of negative roles on a group. Following the laughter, I give each person two positive roles for use when discussing the topic for the evening. A closing evaluation of this session shows that members have come to experience the value of positive roles. They see how such roles enhance the quality of discussion and bring about a closer fellowship.

LEARNING FROM EVALUATIONS

It should be assumed that after an innovation is introduced, there will be an evaluation of it effectiveness. It should not be assumed that the adoption of an innovation means that it is a finished act and that the task force can quit.

By adopting the stance "do it, fix it, try it," the task force learns from the trial and then takes further action in relatively small steps. Doing something and evaluating the results makes it possible to learn quickly from an action.

At the very outset, a task force should determine what criteria they will use for evaluating the innovation. Certainly it will involve more than counting how many turn out for an event.

An important criterion is determining whether or not the innovation moves people toward their desired outcome. Having determined what their criterion will be, they then determine who conducts the evaluation and how it will be used.

One way to evaluate the effectiveness of an innovation is to interview people who have had some exposure to it. The questions asked should be ones agreed to by the task force. Once answers are available, they can be shared and evaluated with other members of the task force. Evaluating an innovation is a learning experience because each one is trying to determine what makes a difference in the lives of people.

During these times of sharing, members of the task force can determine what should remain of an innovation and what should be modified. This is a good procedure. Edward Glaser espouses the following principle: "An innovation will last longer if it is divisible, that is, parts of it may be sustained while other parts drop out."[5]

Another useful way to evaluate an innovation is to distribute a short questionnaire and ask for a quick response. The items might simply ask: "What about the innovation did you feel was strong? What did you feel was weak? What suggestions do you have?" A questionnaire such as this gives people a chance to contribute their insights and feel they have some ownership in the shaping of a new program or procedure. Richard Hutcheson observes:

> For reasons connected with the uniqueness of the church, the most important source of evaluative judgments is the pew. For most Christians the local congregation is the natural habitat of the Holy Spirit. When the collective judgment of many is used the personal bias of individual persons disappears.[6]

Evaluation within a congregation must involve both the human and the divine dimensions. It is not enough to sense what people think or say. There is a need also to discern what the Lord of the church might have to say. Though we may be innovative with respect to style of ministry, care must be taken to not alter its substance. Hence, the process of evaluating also includes a time of prayer, of listening for the guidance of the Holy Spirit.

LEARNING THROUGH IN-SERVICE TRAINING

Pastors often find that it is easier to do a task than to ask someone else to do it. The danger in such an approach is that more and more activities fall on the shoulders of the pastor, creating fatigue and a sense of being overwhelmed. Worse yet, when the pastor does it all, members of the congregation are not learning to do the work of lay ministers.

One of the surprises in the Innovation Study was to discover the benefits accruing to an organization that seeks to equip members through in-service training. The effects of learning opportunities made available by a congregation or service unit are impressive.

Three items in the survey, all dealing with in-service training, clustered to form the scale in sidebar 10.2. It proved to be a strong predictor of an innovative organization and an indicator of internal growth among its leaders. Strong evidence for the predictive power of this measure showed up for congregations in the study. Those scoring high tended to show the following characteristics:

- Church staffs received training in specialized areas.
- Specialists were brought in for occasional meetings with youth leaders to discuss areas of special concern.
- Periodic training sessions were held for volunteer leaders.
- The youth group is referred to as a caring community.[7]

It is impressive to find that when training is emphasized in congregations, one tends to find a caring youth group whose members go out of their way to make strangers feel welcome. One also finds that such training is an ongoing feature in the lives of staff and volunteer leaders of these congregations. This is significant because where training is emphasized, one tends to find an innovativeness that results in few but lasting innovations.[8]

A task force intent on the creation of a new emphasis or ministry should encourage in-service training as an important feature of their innovation.[9] It is a way by which the group can truly foster learning. Members can attend seminars or workshops related to their area of investigation and visit congregations where good things are happening. Books and magazines on their subject of interest should be made available. All these help a task force become a learning unit.

As task force members learn and become informed about their area of innovation, they develop expertise as lay leaders in their congregation. And this is the intent of churches that encourage a cultivation culture.

The pastor has much to say about whether or not there are training opportunities. Such training ought not, though budgeted, be considered an expendable activity, one for which the funds can be spent elsewhere when there is a financial shortfall. On the contrary, training should be viewed as an essential ministry of the church by which lay members are enabled to become little Christs.

Carl George, in *Prepare Your Church for the Future*, notes that the tendency in churches trying to become more progressive is to lean more heavily on their paid staff. On the contrary, he says, every pastor should sum up each week's activities by asking, "To what extent did I contribute to the making of ministers who care for our constituency and those beyond our constituency in the name of Jesus Christ?"[10]

Edgar Schein observes that people in an organization, not least those serving on a task force, regard as important signals what their leader (pastor) pays attention to and rewards. A pastor should be seen as truly concerned about the cultivation of lay ministers' gifts. Then pastors, lay leaders, and members can delight in the emergence of gifts that enrich the life of the congregation.

Some pastors are seen as primarily concerned about who gets the credit for good things that happen in the congregation. When that is true, little will be done to encourage the development of lay leadership. Whichever approach is favored by a pastor, the attitude will be conveyed in subtle ways that members discern.

A pastor needs to be personally convinced that it is a good thing that people in the congregation learn how to address complex issues, think theologically, and bring about significant changes in the ministry of a congregation. A pastor will reveal his or her values by supporting additional training opportunities for task force members.

LEARNING THROUGH GOD'S GUIDANCE

Most of the 350,000 congregations in the United States have a church council or board. This group can become a learning team that models how the people of God seek God's guidance when doing his work. An example of a developing learning team is seen in a rapidly growing black congregation in Carson, California, that was identified as exemplary through the Effective Christian Education Study. This church, First Lutheran, began as a congregation of only twenty people and within ten years had grown to a membership of three hundred.

When visiting this congregation, the research team was impressed by the church council's sensitivity to the guidance of God's Holy Spirit. As one member said, "We are a spiritual church. When our church council is meeting and discussing some aspect of business, it often happens that someone says, 'Let's pray about this.' Then we stop our meeting and have a time of prayer." For these people, council meetings are uplifting times.

This, however, is not how a large number of church councils operate. When Presbyterian Research Services conducted a survey of 605 elders who had just finished their three-year term of office, they found that 29 percent said they were weary and burned out. When asked what was discussed or shared at their council meetings, with fourteen choices being given, the one ranking lowest was "sharing faith stories."[11]

One thing I noticed in the report on minority congregations, singled out as exemplary in the Effective Christian Education Study was their emphasis on prayer. The visiting researchers reported this as a notable characteristic of nineteen out of the twenty-two congregations. By way of contrast, the study found that no more than ten out of the twenty-five Anglo congregations singled out as exemplary in the study were seen as placing a strong emphasis on prayer. I suspect these minority congregations do a better job of seeking God's guidance and teaching reliance on his promises.

Charles Olsen, whose goal is the renewal and revitalization of church boards across America, has heard a high level of frustration and even disillusionment among laypeople with their experience on church boards. Much of this disappointment is due to a missing element—spirituality. New members expect a church-board term to provide an opportunity to develop and deepen their faith. Too often they encounter meetings where in corporate style they hear a litany of reports held together by "book-end prayers." No attempt is made to integrate spirituality and administration.

Through a grant from Lilly Endowment, Olsen was able to test an approach for transforming church boards that incorporates four practices into its meetings: story telling, biblical reflection, prayerful discernment, and visioning the future. His experiences with this approach form the basis for his book *Transforming Church Boards into Communities of Spiritual Leaders.*

Through this project, he has become increasingly aware of a "hunger" in churches to "do board differently." More importantly, he found that his model works. Participants report an increase in positive, open attitudes and three times greater use of spiritual disciplines. He finds also that references to God's presence and to one's personal faith occur twice as often with his approach than typifies traditional church board meetings.

The most satisfying aspect of this emphasis on seeking God's guidance was finding out that boards so involved were working more closely and harmoniously to accomplish meaningful work. Members coming together no longer saw themselves as a gathering of individuals with business to transact but rather as stewards of the community of faith, the church, and its life and ministry.[12]

It is in learning how to discern God's guidance that members of a task force or ministry team grow spiritually. This should be the goal. When coming together for the task of bringing about a significant change in the congregation's ministry, God should be seen as an active participant. When God is seen as alive and active in the planning and activities of members, we find a growing congregation.

It is with this point of view that I have answered the question being raised by pastors and lay leaders: "How do I best introduce the changes required by my congregation for meeting today's emerging needs?" Though the seven steps discussed in this book are important for achieving positive change, the steps require more than human effort. They require the power gained through God's intervention

As a human and divine institution, a congregation over time can develop a readiness to respond quickly to needed change. It can become an instrument of God's Holy Spirit, carrying out the mission made explicit in the life and ministry of Jesus Christ.

Reflection:
On Becoming a Learning Team

• Have we as a team moved beyond dependence on a leader?

• Have we sensed the guidance of God's Spirit in the evaluations we have received?

• What have we learned about ministry and the dynamics of change?

• Have our meetings been times of spiritual growth as we looked to God for guidance?

THE INNOVATION STUDY

BELOW IS A MORE COMPLETE DESCRIPTION of the study that provided the research that informs this book and serves as the basis for the conceptual model.

DAVIS'S THEORY OF CHANGING

The study used the theoretical model of Howard Davis to identify the range of likely factors that might be involved in facilitating change. His review of the twelve hundred best research studies on change led him to develop a conceptual model composed of eight factors listed in the next section. These, he found, encompassed all major considerations in effecting change. His model is unique because it represents a theory of changing, that is, it attempts to explain how change is brought about. Most theories of change are spectator theories. They attempt to explain what has happened or will happen if certain situations occur.

The eight factors that form his behavioral model define very well the elements that any pastor or leader faces when trying to introduce a new hymnal or launch a building drive. The questions given in the next section are based on Davis's conceptual model. They are the ones a pastor might ask when considering whether or not to introduce a major innovation or change into a congregation. They illustrate the range of factors found in his conceptual model.

DAVIS'S CONCEPTUAL MODEL

Ability. Does our congregation have the resources and capabilities to implement and carry out what is being proposed? Significant obstacles would be a lack of qualified leaders, funds, or facilities, and people being too busy.

Values. Is what is being proposed consistent with the values and beliefs of this congregation? Significant obstacles here would be peoples discomfort with the values underlying the program, disagreement among members over goals of the congregation, or unthinking adherence to tradition.

Idea. Is the idea behind the proposal sufficiently known and understood? The members may be inadequately informed, the innovation may be misunderstood, and not enough time may have been given for consideration of the proposal.

Circumstances. Do the circumstances that surround us—our internal and external environment—support what is being proposed? A change in leadership may jeopardize the program. An unusual circumstance could force postponement. A decision "from above" (top administrators) could stop everything.

Timing. In light of current events, is this the best time to introduce this change? Consider the priorities and program already set for the year, what the leaders have already committed themselves to do, and the time we have for necessary feedback and modification

Obligation. Do the people in a position to influence a change feel a need for that change? The proposed change will be hindered if few know the congregation's mission or goals, or see the need for what is being proposed, or think the innovation duplicates present programs.

Resistances. Is there a perceptible disinclination to change, a manifest disinterest or vocal opposition? Manifestations of this resistance may be lack of confidence in the ability to manage the change, a fear of loss of power or control, or expressions that what is proposed is really not needed.

Yield. Are members sufficiently aware of the benefits, the potential rewards that will come as a result of this innovation? Obstacles to being convinced of a favorable outcome are attitudes such as these: a feeling that this innovation won't work, a feeling that too much time is required for what is gained, and a proneness to criticize whatever is not an instant success.

A review of these questions shows how completely the Davis model identifies the range of considerations for launching a major innovation. Its comprehensiveness made it a useful domain definition for the first step in our research project.

DEVELOPING SURVEY ITEMS

Our next step was to interview leaders of the five participating national youth organizations to gain from them concrete, specific descriptions (items) of what happens in an organization to either facilitate or hinder making needed change.

The five participating youth organizations were the National Catholic Education Association, 4-H Extension, Camp Fire Inc., United Methodist Church, and the American Lutheran Church. They assisted in the development of a pool of items that would reflect every facet of the Davis model. Through their cooperation an initial pool of several hundred items was developed through group interviews (focus groups) and personal conversations as well as through reviews of the literature. The resultant items were tested by staff persons of these partner organizations for omissions or inappropriateness for their organization.

Next, the items were field tested on 218 persons from the five participating organizations. An item analysis of their response to each item and written comments provided a basis for dropping or revising items. The end result was an instrument of 153 items now ready for a national survey because the instrument reflected the full range of people's attitudes toward changes an organization may introduce.

COLLECTING AND ANALYZING SURVEY DATA

A national survey was carried out in 1977 involving 2,261 respondents from 191 randomly selected clubs, schools, congregations, or youth groups in the five participating organizations. Respondents used the 153-item instrument to describe what they observed as hindering or facilitating change in their local organization. Data resulting from their responses were analyzed by means of a variety of computer, multivariate processes.

It should be noted that the local organizations drawn into the study were selected randomly from memberships lists of the five national organizations. A total of 365 local units were randomly selected, and 191 agreed to participate. Five policy makers, five staff people, and five volunteer program leaders participated by answering the survey items in a group administered situation. Thus, an average of fifteen persons in each local group participated in the study.

Our analysis of the survey data by means of factor and cluster analysis showed an interesting fact of life. People in organizations as contrasting in style and purpose as our five cosponsors have nevertheless similar ideas of how an organization should function. Their ideas regarding organizational functioning (constructs they hold unconsciously) became evident in the way their responses formed distinct patterns. Their patterned responses caused items to intercorrelate and form twenty distinct clusters of items. Significantly, we could identify the construct underlying each patterned response by reading the items found in each cluster. The construct reflected in these items served in skewer-like fashion as their unifying motif.

DEVELOPING A READINESS-FOR-CHANGE INSTRUMENT

To develop a readiness-for-change instrument, we formed scales from the twenty clusters of items. We did this in order to measure the extent to which each construct was characteristic of people in the study.

Once we had formed these scales, the entire body of survey data was processed again to derive scale scores instead of percentage responses to individual items. Twenty scale scores for every individual in the study made it possible to carry out a second order factor analysis. This procedure allowed the twenty clusters (or scales) to group empirically into families of scales. We found that the scales intercorrelated with each other to form five separate families, which we came to regard as dynamic factors.

One might wonder, "What was the unifying factor that caused these scales to group together into families of scales?" The answer to this question is found in the way our respondents answered the 153 items. Unconsciously, they reflected patterns of thought as they answered the items. These patterned responses (detectable only by computer) caused certain scales to correlate with other scales to form each family. Determining these patterns of thought were the convictions people held about how an organization should function.

What are these convictions? Answers can be inferred by noting the subject matter that characterizes the scales (or clusters) within each family. The five that emerged relate to an organization's atmosphere, its group skills, its values, its resistances, and its motivation. They are five factors these adults deem important for a successful organization. They are ones held unconsciously in the minds of people when they consider what is needed to be an innovative organization. The five factors deemed important by people in service organizations are essentially these:

- an organizational atmosphere conducive to change
- group skill in knowing how to introduce a change
- values that give priority to growth
- freedom from attitudes that hinder or immobilize progress
- a desire for change motivated by concern

Note that these factors emerged from the perceptions of adults serving in the five youth-serving organizations. Because the adults in the study were a national, random sample and the survey instrument they used provided a comprehensive list of change items, it is reasonable to conclude that these resulting five factors are the ones intuitively held by people in most groups, including congregations.

Evidence to support the application of these findings to congregations came when separate factor analyses were carried out for the adults of each of the five organizations. We discovered that the resulting families of scales for each organization were essentially the same. This is noteworthy because three of the five national organizations had a Christian orientation and the other two a basically secular one.

As will be noted, the five factors identified above figure prominently in the conceptual model that forms the outline for this book. They identify forces a pastor or leader of a congregation can use to enhance the likelihood of success when introducing a significant change or innovation. And second, they identify qualities that over time create an organizational readiness to respond spontaneously to emerging needs. Readiness of this kind reduces the response time members need for launching ministries that address twenty-first-century tragedies.

TESTING THE VALIDITY OF THE MEASURES

We tested the validity of our measures and found they predict innovativeness, that is, an organization's ability to carry out its mission.

To establish our case, however, it was necessary to carry out a validation study. We began by identifying innovativeness as an expression of readiness. Having done so, we met with leaders of each participating national organization to determine how innovativeness is expressed in their organization. We found that what is innovative activity for one group, however, is not so for another. Therefore, it was necessary to define and measure innovativeness separately for each group. This meant that separate instruments, with one exception, had to be developed to measure the innovativeness of groups within each national organization. The exception was that the two church groups could use the same instrument.

The measures of innovativeness we developed for each group consisted of items describing activities, processes, or programs found to be innovative within each organization.

To establish the idea that organizations scoring positively on these scales are innovative, we collected the following validation data. We returned three years following the original 1977 study to collect information from the youth organizations that participated originally. We gave their adult leaders the Readiness for Change instrument of 153 items they took in 1977. In addition, we gave the Innovativeness instrument to three outside judges (people not in the original study).These were people who knew what had happened in their local organization during the intervening three years. They identified the innovative steps their group had taken to overcome obstacles, address needs and move their organization toward achieving its mission and goals.

Now we had excellent data for addressing the issue of validity. The issue can be posed by this question: "Can one legitimately infer that each of the twenty scales measures what the scale purports to measure?" If one can say yes to this question on the basis of validating information, then one can identify each scale as a characteristic of innovativeness.

To secure the information needed to answer this question, we correlated the 1977 Readiness for Change scores with the 1980–1981 innovativeness items (used by the three judges to describe innovative activity in their organization). We predicted that groups scoring high on a each scale or construct in 1977 would, during the intervening three years, have been involved in innovative activity similar to activity described in that scale. Because our prediction for each scale was confirmed, we could claim predictive validity for the twenty scales. (Documentation for this is included in the publication *Five Shaping Forces*, pages II, 4–10.)

Next, we correlated the Readiness for Change scores from the 1980–1981 survey with the innovativeness items. This procedure provided another kind of validating information. We found that groups scoring high on a given scale in 1980–81 were engaged in innovative activity related to that construct and groups scoring low were not. These data enabled us to establish a strong case for what is known as construct validity. Thus we gained an empirical basis for claiming that sixteen of our scales assess innovativeness and four assess resistance to such activity. Based on this evidence, we concluded that there is good reason to assume that the five factors identified in this book (of which the twenty measures are constituent elements) are strong indicators of an organization's readiness to act.

GROUP ROLES

HOW CAN ONE SERVE or destroy a group? There is an undeniable witness or impression a person makes in a group. This impression, though made unconsciously, is as real to others as a fragrance. Below are ways a person can be of service to a group or tear a group apart.

HOW TO HELP WELD A GROUP TOGETHER

1. Encourager
- Speak words that reveal an appreciation for the other person's point of view.
- Say things that show enthusiasm.
- Show interest in everybody's comments, even those less important, by listening intently.

2. Tension Reliever
- Act like a host to strangers who are present.
- Make pleasant comments that are appropriate and that everybody enjoys.
- Address uncooperative people in a way that shows tolerance and acceptance.

3. Harmonizer
- Try to show how differing points of view might be brought together.
- Demonstrate agreement to someone else's idea and try to strengthen it.

4. Follower
If silent, show that you are following along by demonstrating your interest. This can be done nonverbally in ways as simple as the following:
- Sitting with the group
- Leaning forward while listening
- Looking at each person who speaks
- Reacting in some way as discussion progresses (for example, smiling, nodding head)

5. Reaction Observer

- Tell what the group feeling seems to be or describe what the group's reaction appears to be to certain ideas.
- Notice who is not participating and try to involve the person in some way.

HOW TO AID DISCUSSION AND INCREASE INTEREST

1. Initiator or Energizer

- Break the ice if no one is talking by giving a suggestion or proposing an idea.
- Stimulate the group to action or a decision.
- Suggest ways the group might act.

2. Opinion Seeker/Giver

- Ask others what they think about a certain problem or idea, and in that way stimulate discussion and involve others.
- Be willing to give your frank opinion so the group knows what you think about the topic.

3. Goal Setter

- Call attention to the goal and relate discussion to that goal.

4. Summarizer

- Listen for related ideas or suggestions so you can integrate or pull together the group's ideas.
- Help the group progress toward a solution by summarizing the thoughts expressed by different individuals.

5. Elaborator

- Try to show understanding of someone else by rephrasing or restating the contribution.
- Give examples that develop meaning. Clarify proposals by trying to envision how they would work out if adopted.

6. Information Seeker/Giver

- Ask for clarification and more information. Offer information.

HOW TO TEAR A GROUP APART

1. Dominator
   • Assert yourself strongly with authority or superiority. Give directions or interrupt the contributions of others.

2. Recognition Seeker
   • Attempt to call attention to yourself by loud or excessive talking, extreme ideas, unusual behavior. Act in ways that say, "I must be noticed at any cost."
   • Vie with others to produce the best ideas, talk the most, gain favor with the leader, and impress the group.

3. Blocker
   • Disagree and oppose beyond reason. Try to bring up an issue after the group has dropped it.
   • Argue too much on a point and reject certain ideas without consideration.
   • Insist on your own point of view.

4. Antagonizer
   • Withdraw from the group by not paying attention to what people are saying, day-dreaming, whispering to others, or purposely slighting certain members in the group and making them feel unwanted.
   • Act as though everything were childish and unimportant.

5. Aggressor
   • Reveal a critical, sarcastic attitude by edged remarks or biting retorts.
   • Show disagreement by expressing astonishment or disbelief toward comments in a disparaging way.
   • Make attempts to deflate someone else or override the opinions of others.

6. Playboy
   • Clown, joke, mimic, or disrupt the work of the group.

7. Cry Baby
   • Make frequent statements of dissatisfaction or disappointment.
   • Act like you are on the defensive or very sensitive to a hint of criticism.

NOTES

THE CHANGE FACTORS presented in this book became a research project for me one afternoon in Colorado when I was seated on a park table overlooking Cottonwood Lake, a turquoise liquid jewel in the setting of the Wasatch mountains west of Buena Vista. Alongside me was a man I admired, Howard Davis, then chief of a division in the National Institute of Mental Health. He had asked me to meet him there because he wanted to interest me in the subject of change. He chose the setting because of his great love for the Colorado mountains.

In this setting, hearing faintly in the distance the sounds of elk calling to one another, I focused on him as he wondered out loud about an area of special interest to him. Would it be possible, he asked, to identify through a research project an institution's readiness to make significant changes?

I was intrigued with his agenda and the possibilities of such a project. While admiring this gorgeous setting, I heard him suggest that I submit a proposal for a project that would identify factors facilitating or hindering institutional change.

As a research scientist, my chief qualification for tackling this complex issue centered in my strong interest in the subject, something Davis had noticed. He knew of my concern while serving as president of Search Institute that our research for youth-serving organizations truly impact youth leaders and ultimately youth themselves. He knew how this concern shaped our research and motivated us to effect some of the changes called for by our findings. Significantly, we had already in 1970 identified our institute as an agency of change.

Howie, as we affectionately called him, began describing some of the elements he thought should be included in a study on change. With pen and paper in hand, I scribbled frantically the essence of his provocative ideas for breaking open this unexamined issue. The notes I took became the basis for a proposal I submitted to the National Institute of Mental Health. It reflected many of the hopes expressed by Howie Davis that afternoon in Colorado.

Once the proposal was funded, it was not long before codirector Shelby Andress and I were deeply involved in a subject that has engaged our professional efforts for over twenty years. The project itself, extended through a supplementary grant, became a $750,000 research effort taking six years to complete. It involved 356 youth organizations randomly drawn from five national youth-serving organizations. As a result of this project we gained unprecedented data for identifying the factors of change presented in this book.

Part of this research effort involved working with Ronald Lippitt of the University of Michigan. Together with him and Shelby Andress, a group process called Vision-to-Action was developed. This process was designed to help service-oriented groups interpret and act on their own research data. As used today, it enables a group to identify a desired future and develop a plan of action for bringing their vision into being. Shelby, as director of consulting services for Search Institute, has used this Vision-to-Action process with hundreds of mental health, educational, religious, and service groups throughout the country. (I have also used the process to a lesser degree.)

IMPORTANT FEATURES OF THE INNOVATION STUDY

National Scope. The study involved 2,261 professional staff, volunteer program leaders, and policy makers who were actively involved in 191 local organizations randomly selected from the rosters of five national youth serving organizations: United Methodist Church, American Lutheran Church, National Catholic Educational Association, 4-H Extension, and Campfire Girls.

Focus on Change. The study's purpose was to assess an organization's readiness to innovate. This meant identifying the factors present in a group that would facilitate the making of needed change or hinder this process. The twofold purpose of the study was to develop an instrument that could assess an organization's readiness for change and to devise strategies a consultant might use when introducing an innovative program or process.

Questionnaire Comprehensiveness. Using Howard Davis's theory for change and the guided observations of 218 people who served in the member organizations, we formulated a pool of items that describe obstacles an organization faces when introducing an innovation. These items, once pared down to 153, provided the means by which the 2,261 randomly selected respondents could describe how their local organization coped with change. The questionnaire served us well because it touched all the key areas involved in change except two idiosyncratic ones: timing and unique circumstances.

Longitudinal Feature. A unique and important feature of this study was being able to return three years after the first survey to give the questionnaire a second time. During this return visit, we were able to collect information on innovative activities that had occurred for each group during the three years between surveys. This additional information enabled us to determine which factors (as measured by the surveys) were associated with innovative activities and which factors were associated with resistance to change. Thankfully, this longitudinal feature enabled us to establish a case for claiming both concurrent and predictive validity for the factors found in our conceptual model. This is a very important feature of the study.

Innovativeness Defined. In order to assess the innovativeness of the 191 local organizations during the three-year period between surveys, we needed a measure of innovativeness. We defined it as "something new or different that is introduced into the program, process, or structure of an organization in order to solve problems or advance its mission." We needed a measure of innovativeness that independent judges (people not involved in the two surveys) could use in describing the innovative activities they had seen adopted in their group or organization. In developing this measure, we discovered that innovative activity in one national organization is very different from innovative activity in another. Therefore, it became necessary to develop separate measures appropriate for each group. Only the United Methodists and

Lutherans shared an understanding of what constitutes innovative activity in a youth group.

Extent of Cooperation. Of the 365 local organizations invited to participate in the study, a total of 191 (53 percent) did cooperate. We asked that in each participating group, five staff, five volunteer program leaders, and five policy makers take the survey both times. In addition, we asked that three judges in each unit be identified who would know what kinds of innovative activities were adopted during the three-year period. The reason for choosing eighteen people who were intimately acquainted with the local agency and not selecting a random sample of members was clear. We wanted the evaluations of what happens in an organization to be made by people most aware of its life and struggles.The fifteen who took the surveys represented the inner circle of people who knew best the obstacles being faced in their organization whenever an innovation was introduced. The three who served as independent judges identified the innovative activity of their unit but did not take the survey.

Data Analysis. Interestingly, we found through our analysis of the survey data that people in organizations as contrasting in style and purpose as our cosponsors still hold similar ideas about what an organization should do or be. This became evident in the way the participants answered the 153 survey items. Their responses tended to form consistent patterns. As a result of their patterned responses, we found upon analysis that the items intercorrelated to form clusters. Significantly, the items in each cluster described an idea or construct. The phenomenon is that respondents held this construct unconsciously, and the construct caused respondents to give responses that fell into a pattern. The pattern of responses caused the items to intercorrelate.

The twenty resulting clusters of items formed scales that have proven to be reliable, valid, and useful in assessing the readiness of an organization to introduce change. The group profiles formed by these scales are being used by consultants to identify whether or not a group is ready for a major change such as taking on a building drive. (For a description of the validity of the instrument's twenty scales, see Appendix A. The scales, which have an average of five items each, yield an average reliability coefficient of 0.72. The publication *Five Shaping Forces* presents the evidence for being able to claim both predictive and concurrent validity. See chapter 2, pages 3, 6–9. For a more extensive explanation of procedures used to design and implement this study, see Appendix A.)

CHAPTER ONE

1. Reports on ten- and fifteen-year trend analyses involving both public school youth and church youth are found in my book *Five Cries of Youth*, xiv–xviii. Another reference is the report on trends in moral and social behaviors of Americans found in Bennett's article "Redeeming the Time." A third reference regarding the incidence of at-risk behaviors among youth of six major Protestant denominations is the book by my wife, Irene, and me, *Five Cries of Parents*, 115.

2. This quote is from "A Rough Draft of a Vision Statement," written by Rev. Peter Strommen for his congregation, November 23, 1993.

3. Bosch, *Transforming Mission*, 10.

4. Hutcheson, *Wheel within the Wheel*, 192.

5. Warren, *The Purpose Driven Church*, 60.

6. Hale and Williams, *Managing Change*, 1.

7. Kuenning's scholarly presentation provides documentation for the innovativeness and openness that was present among Lutheran congregations of the pre–Civil War period. See *Rise and Fall of American Lutheran Pietism*, 93, 97.

8. Glaser, Abelson, and Garrison, *Putting Knowledge to Use*, 9, 10.

9. Callahan, *Twelve Keys to an Effective Church*, 68.

10. It was this question and concern for organizational readiness that precipitated the research foundational to this book. This question intrigued the sponsor of the research, Howard Davis of the National Institute of Mental Health, whose dream was to use his office for funding projects to help the poor and desolate. His final criterion for evaluating a proposed project was a simple one: "How will this help Mrs Swanson?"—a mythical, distressed, and downtrodden person whose picture hung on his wall. As a result of his deep concern for troubled people he wondered, "How can an organization's readiness to act be increased and made more responsive to the tragic situations that surround them?"

11. Senge, *The Fifth Discipline*, 14, 69. The fifth discipline to which Senge refers is "systems thinking." He refers to "component technologies" as useful when they converge into a systematic approach so members are continually learning. He calls for a shift from seeing people as helpless reactors to seeing them as active participants in shaping their reality, from reacting to the present to creating the future. Because his approach reinforces the conceptual model being used in this book, frequent references will be made to his book.

12. Lippitt, "Utilizing Resistance as a Resource for Change," 1–2.

13. The Vision-to-Action process was developed as part of the research project that serves as a basis for this book. It is a carefully structured workshop approach involving two four-hour sessions. During the workshop a planning group evaluates data on its external and internal environment, arrives at a vision of its desired future, and begins the process of making plans to bring their vision into being. It is a process that has been used effectively with hundreds of schools, colleges, mental health institutions, hospitals, congregations, and agencies.

CHAPTER TWO

1. There are other puzzling factors besides tradition posed by questions such as the following: Why do individuals within a congregation vary so markedly in their willingness to consider innovations needed to meet emerging needs? Why are people living in certain parts of the country more resistive to change than others? Why does it take so long for some people to open their mind to the need for a proposed program?

Answers to these questions about personality, regional, and affiliation differences will come from two major sources: (1) published studies in the field of innovation and change, and (2) books written by consultants in the field of organizational change who work with religious or business institutions.

2. The Innovation Study included youth and adults from two secular organizations (4-H Extension and Campfire Girls) and three religious

organizations (United Methodist, Lutheran, and Roman Catholic). These contrasting samples enabled us to make comparisons regarding factors that hinder or facilitate change in either secular or religious groups. When we factor analyzed the two samples (that is, allowed the data to organize themselves with respect to underlying factors) we found that approximately the same human factors emerged for both groups, meaning the same underlying dynamics characterized both the church and nonchurch samples.

3. Because he finds innovativeness to be a continuous variable, he partitions adopters into discrete categories using the parameters of a normal curve.

4. He uses this conceptual device because he has found that adopter distributions closely approach normality. Using the two statistics of mean and standard deviation, he divides a normal distribution into five categories: innovators, early adopters, early majority, late majority, and laggards.

5. Rogers, *Diffusion of Innovations*, 248.

6. Rogers, *Communication Technology*, 134.

7. Rogers, *Diffusion of Innovations*, 241.

8. I am grateful to Paul Kentz, a former graduate student of mine who is now mission and ministry facilitator for the Texas District of the Lutheran Church—Missouri Synod. He helped identify people in the early church who resemble the roles of innovator, early adopter, later adopter, and laggards.

9. Daniel Goleman, *Emotional Intelligence*, 215 and 217.

10. Rogers, *Communication Technology*, 154.

11. Benson and Williams, *Religion on Capitol Hill*, 217.

12. Johnson and Sampson, eds., *Religion*, 200.

13. Ibid. 45.

14. Senge, *The Fifth Discipline*, 364.

15. Wink, *Unmasking the Powers*, 1.

16. Hutcheson, *Wheel within the Wheel*, 25.

17. Machiavelli, *The Prince*, 51.

18. Davis, "Change and Innovation," 1.

19. Rogers, *Diffusion of Innovations*, 8–9.

CHAPTER THREE

1. Callahan, *Effective Church Leadership*, 210.

2. Waterman, *Adhocracy*, 19–21.

3. Senge, *The Fifth Discipline*, 4, 13.

4. Goleman, *Emotional Intelligence*, 151.

5. In the Catholic schools scoring high on this scale, visitors were impressed by the friendly reception given them; teachers said they felt they are part of a larger mission; teachers were given extra time for professional growth; parents rallied to support the school; and teachers showed they are anxious for their students to succeed.

In the Methodist and Lutheran congregations scoring high on Organizational Pride, exuberance was manifested when people gathered; get-togethers were marked by a wide participation of people, frequent bursts of singing, and laughing; and there were reports of groups performing outside the congregation and a remarkable willingness of members to volunteer.

6. Kouzes and Posner, *The Leadership Challenge*, 221.

CHAPTER FOUR

1. Hutcheson, *Wheel within the Wheel*, 156.

2. Because this chapter makes frequent reference to the perception of members, readers may wonder about the accuracy of people's perception of their pastor's style of leadership, as well as other aspects of congregational life.

We wondered too. So we compared the perceptions of the three groups of people we had in the Innovation Study—staff, policy makers, and program leaders. Interestingly, all three groups showed similar perceptions of their organization's openness and resistance on most of the measures. To us this was significant, inasmuch as volunteers are in and out, touching base only occasionally with their organization. Yet what they sense and observe usually agrees with what full-time staff report about their organization. Apparently, an organization has a life and quality of its own that has continuity over time. Apparently, too, these organizational qualities are sensed quite accurately and perceived by even the infrequent visitor. Hence, the perceptions of members are worth taking seriously.

3. Schneider, "Productivity Improvement," 10–12.

4. Benson, Roehlkepartain, and Andress, *Congregations at Crossroads*, 34.

5. Schneider, "Productivity Improvement," 12–16.

6. Olson, "Learning from Lyle Schaller," 82–83.

7. Klaas and Brown, *Church Membership Initiative*, 5.

8. Schneider, "Productivity," 16–19.

9. Olson,"Learning from Lyle Schaller," 82–83.

10. Schneider, "Productivity Improvement," 19–22.

11. Klaas and Brown, *Church Membership Initiative*, 10.

12. Kouzes and Posner, *Leadership Challenge*, 21.

13. Goleman, *Emotional Intelligence*, 88–89.

14. Glaser, Abelson, and Garrison, in *Putting Knowledge to Use*, 76, discuss several studies that show how morale is related to organizational innovativeness.

15. Lippitt, Benne, and Havelock found that teachers who perceived their principal as being supportive of innovation did in fact innovate more. Also, they found that more than one-third of the teachers to whom the principal brought educational literature and called their attention to new practices did adopt them, whereas those who lacked this encouragement did not adopt any new practices. (See Glaser, Abelson, and Garrison, *Putting Knowledge to Work*, 115. This book is a distillation from the comprehensive literature that reports findings from studies on knowledge utilization and innovative change. It reviews the writings of academics and practitioners from sociology and social work, political science and government, economics and business management, education and communication, anthropology, mental health, and systems analysis.)

16. The list of criteria started with twelve hundred general descriptions of ministry which through screening and pretest procedures were winnowed down to 444 survey items that identified the range of criteria people actually use. Then five thousand lay adults, pastors, and seminary students, randomly selected from within the forty-seven denominations, rated items they deemed most important in a pastor.

When we factor analyzed the resulting data (that is, allowed the data to organize themselves), we found sixty-four clusters of items emerging, each of which described a dimension of ministry. We proceeded with one more step, using second-order factor analysis. We wanted to see if the clusters would form families, in the same way as the items had formed clusters.

The results were provocative. Eleven families of clusters emerged to identify eleven major themes of ministry. These are eleven areas people consider when evaluating the effectiveness of their pastor, irrespective of denomination.

This comprehensive study provided added confidence in people's ability to make insightful evaluations of their pastor's approach to people. The fact that 444 criterion items were identified and used (after extensive screening) underscores the ability of members to be discriminating in their perceptions.

17. Schuller, Strommen, and Brekke, *Ministry in America*, 14–21.
18. Goleman, *Emotional Intelligence*, 45.
19. Ibid. 149.
20. Senge, *The Fifth Discipline*, 172.
21. Glaser, Abelson, and Garrison, *Putting Knowledge to Work*, 61.
22. Senge, *The Fifth Discipline*, 168.
23. Ibid. 285.
24. 4-H groups ranking high on these items did the following:

• Introduced novel and creative ideas in their ways of communicating with leaders.
• Employed creative, new approaches to club tours, fairs, and shows.
• Made special efforts to reach all members of a family.
• Used specially designed programs to reach specific audiences, such as people with disabilities or minority groups.

Jesuit schools and those of the National Catholic Education Association who ranked high on this dimension showed evidences of creative activity in these ways.
• Teachers think it is fun to be at school.
• The faculty stresses critical thinking and freedom of expression.
• Faculty and administration are more likely to see possibilities than problems.
• Staff introduces few but lasting innovations.

25. Senge, *The Fifth Discipline*, 287.
26. Hogan, "Trouble at the Top," 12–13.

CHAPTER FIVE

1. Search Institute, *Your Congregation's Future.*
2. Hulstrand, "Pioneering on the Prairie," 6–7.
3. Niebuhr, "In Isolated U.S. Churches."
4. Ronsvalle and Ronsvalle, "The End of Benevolence?" 1010–1014.
5. Mead, *The Once and Future Church*, 2–50.
6. Nicholi, "Hope in a Secular Age," 112.
7. Monroe, *Finding God at Harvard*, 14, 15, 16.
8. Hunter, *How to Reach Secular People*, 41

9. Strommen, *Research on Religious Development*, xx. This survey of all published research that included the religious variable was replicated years later (1983) with the same results as recorded in this publication. David Larson and his collaborators reviewed articles appearing in four major psychiatric journals (1978–1982) and found that only 59 of the 3,777 quantitative studies included religious variables.

10. Strommen and Strommen, *Five Cries of Parents*, 134.

11. Bennett, "Redeeming Our Time," 3.

12. The Effective Christian Education Study was a research project of Search Institute in Minneapolis, Minnesota. Funded by the Lilly Endowment and the participating denominations, this three-and-a-half year project sought to evaluate and strengthen congregationally based Christian education. It assessed the maturity in faith of adolescents, Christian educators, pastors, and lay adults, as well as their loyalty to congregation and denomination. It identified the features of congregational life, including programming features, that promote faith maturity and loyalty. Data for the study came from respondents within randomly selected congregations of the following six denominations: Christian Church (Disciples of Christ), Evangelical Lutheran Church n America, Presbyterian Church (U.S.A.), United Church of Christ, United Methodist Church, and the Southern Baptist Convention.

13. Glover, DeJesus, and Strommen, *Congregational Site Visit Reports*, 34–41.

14. Warren, *The Purpose Driven Church*, 166–169.

15. Senge, *The Fifth Discipline*, 150.

16. Towns, *Ten of Today's Most Innovative Churches*, 31.

17. Callahan, *Twelve Keys to an Effective Church*, 1.

18. We did wonder, however, whether the contrast in response of these two groups might be credited to contrasts in effectiveness of the two consultants who presented the project each evening. But our evaluative data made of each presentation by trained observers showed that this was not the reason. On the contrary, our evidence showed both consultants to be consistent and equally effective in the way they conducted sessions for all ten groups.

19. The power in a group's awareness of need became evident when we made an analysis of our data using Automatic Interaction Detection (a complex computer analysis). The purpose was to identify which variables (of those entered into the analysis) account for most of the variance in people's adoption of the innovation. To our surprise we found that a feeling of need for what was offered (and subsequently feeling good about the worthwhileness of the meeting) accounted for 27 percent of the variance. This is a very high percentage, especially when many variables are involved in an analysis.

The next highest percentage was 19 percent for the variable "agency affiliation." This we found interesting, for it showed that highly organized groups like Campfire Girls and 4-H youth groups find it difficult to take on new innovations on short notice. Their carefully scheduled goals for the year, their full calendars, and their program commitments make it difficult to take on a new commitment mid-year. It was the less structured and more informally organized congregational groups that found it easier to respond.

Our field experiment provided confirmation for what has been repeatedly observed. To quote authors Glaser, Abelson, and Garrison, "One of the most frequently advocated principles regarding innovation and change is that in order for change to be successful, it must be in response to a felt need" (Glaser, Abelson, and Garrison, *Putting Knowledge to Work*, 167–168).

20. Klaas and Brown, *Church Membership Initiative*, 5.

21. Benson, *Effective Christian Education*, 25.

22. Search Institute in Minneapolis has developed several surveys that are useful in identifying hidden needs. The most recent and useful is "Voices of Faith." This survey does two things. It shows members' evaluations of various dimensions of congregational life. And second, it shows where members are with respect to their faith life. Significantly, the higher members rate their dimensions of congregational life, the higher their faith scores. The two are linked.

23. Hutcheson, *Wheel within the Wheel*, 64–81.

24. Rogers, *Diffusion of Innovations*, 166.

25. Ibid. 167.

CHAPTER SIX

1. Kouzes and Posner, *The Leadership Challenge*, 190–201.

2. Senge, *The Fifth Discipline*, 175.

3. Ibid. 198.

4. Allen, "Church Learns from Bible's Teachings on Tithing."

5. The correlations between these criterion items and the scale measuring Sense of Mission range between 0.49 and 0.54,.and all are significant at a 0.00 level of significance. These correlations, which could not have occurred by chance, indicate the strong association between a sense of mission and innovative activity.

6. Spencer, *Winning Through Participation*, 119.

7. Peters and Waterman, *In Search of Excellence*, 127.

8. Kouzes and Posner, *The Leadership Challenge*, 8.

9. Spencer, *Winning Through Participation*, 142.

10. Hutcheson, *Wheel within the Wheel*, 55, 66.

11. Hadaway, *Church Growth Principles*, 11–113.

12. Shawchuck, et al., *Marketing for Congregations*, 245.

13. Callahan, *Effective Church Leadership*, 19, 22.

14. Shawchuck, et al., *Marketing for Congregations*, 92–93.

15. Ibid. 87, 91.

16. Senge, *The Fifth Discipline*, 206.

17. Barna, *Without a Vision*, 28–29, 39.

18. Hadaway,. *Church Growth Principles*, 98.

19. Ibid. 41, 67, 71.

CHAPTER SEVEN

1. Lippitt, "Utilizing Resistance," 2.

2. Benjamin and Walz,

3. Glaser, Abelson, and Garrison, *Putting Knowledge to Work*, 80, 83.

4. The correlations between this simple scale of three items and criterion items used to evaluate the innovativeness of a school (long-range planning, cost-of-living raises for faculty, and curriculum review) are amazing. The correlations range between 0.78 and 0.81 with the significance level of 0.00, meaning these correlations could not have happened by chance.

5. Lippitt, "Utilizing Resistance," 2.

6. Glaser, Abelson, and Garrison, *Putting Knowledge to Work*, 88.

7. Rogers, *Communication Technology*, 27.

8. In the Innovation Study we found that congregations taking the time to gain this level of involvement, drew from the judges the highest ratings on innovativeness. These congregations were seen as outstanding in the way they made changes to better achieve their purposes.

9. We visited a number of youth-serving organizations to invite cost-free participation in a government-subsidized program of training. Puzzled over the fact that fifteen groups failed to take advantage of a remarkable offer for a highly desirable program, we returned later to interview three respondents from each group. We asked them to identify the reasons their group did not accept the offer. The ones they identified but never voiced when the visiting consultant gave his presentation were obstacles that could have been dealt with if known at the time.

Here are the obstacles volunteered by the thirty-eight people interviewed, listed in order of frequency mentioned:

• *Ability.* We lack the time required by the project,as well as the money, and necessary talents. (33)

• *Need.* We are not sure this is something we really need. (16)

• *Timing.* The idea is fine but is this not a good time for it. (13)

• *Information.* Some did not understand what is being offered. (12)

• *Yield.* We were not sure benefits will equal the time required. (10)

• *Value.* We wonder what difference it will make in our groups effectiveness. (7)

• *Resistance.* Some people felt threatened by this program. (4)

• *Circumstance.* We have too many things in the hopper now. (1)

It is likely that if these obstacles had been voiced when the consultant was present, solutions could have been found or explanations given to have encouraged acceptances from several declining organizations. Task forces can expect legitimizers to have similar questions in mind. It is helpful if mention of these obstacles can be anticipated and addressed.

Another estimate of obstacles to expect came from 2,261 respondents we asked for a written response to an open-ended item stem, "A circumstance that hindered us from making any program changes was _____." Their answers gave us over two thousand descriptions of the kind of obstacles hindering people in service organizations from making a program change. A content analysis of a random sample of 706 written responses gave us the following information:

Obstacle	Frequency Mentioned
Finances	120
Preference for status quo	78
Limited number of staff	64
Lack of time	51
Negative attitudes of leaders	48
Lack of parental support	41
Lack of interest- apathy	41
Negative attitudes of youth	37
Lack of resource people	33
Lack of space	31

One can assume that finances will loom big in people's minds. The other obstacles listed above represent the kinds of resistance normal to most any endeavor.

10. The eighteen agencies whose executive adamantly refused to participate earlier in the field experiment did later take the Readiness for Change survey. We found they measured no higher on the Resistance scales or lower on the Innovative Attitude scales than the thirty-eight agencies that earlier participated in the study. Thus, we learned that groups ought not be labeled as less ready for innovation simply because their chief executive denies cooperation.

11. Correlations with the measure Internal Tension and items listed in the text range between 0.50 and 0.70, to indicate the devastating effect of internal tension on any organization.

CHAPTER EIGHT

1. Carlzon, *Moments of Truth*, 26–29, 113.
2. Zaltman and Duncan, *Strategies for Planned Change*
3. Luecke, *The Other Story*, 2, 9–18.
4. This account of Our Saviour's Lutheran Church is based on an interview of one of its pastors, Rev. Janet Tiedeman, in January 1997. The congregation continued its full program by using the facilities of neighboring churches, the Lutheran Social Service agency building, and a nearby school.
5. Senge, *The Fifth Discipline*, 208, 218, 221.
6. The importance of a listening stance is shown in the fact that the criterion items for innovativeness listed in the text showed correlations with the scale Listening for Needs that ranged from 0.63 to 0.77. These are exceptionally high.
7. Note what were distinguishing features of parochial schools whose faculty and staff placed a high value on such involvement.

National Catholic Education Association parochial schools

TEACHERS	• spend extra time helping students
	• are given extra time for professional growth
	• are eager for students to succeed
	• collaborate with colleagues in classroom planning
PARENTS:	• show up for student conferences
	• rally to provide support for the school
	• are satisfied with the education their children receive
	• are very appreciative of the school
	• show a less formal attitude toward clergy and religious

Congregational Youth Groups (Methodist and Lutheran)

ADULT LEADERS	• are involved in periodic training sessions
	• are always open to new ideas, materials, and programs
YOUTH	• turn out in large percentages for weekend retreats

The correlations between a high value on involvement and each description of innovative activity could not have occurred by accident once in a hundred, which points out the power resident in the phenomenon of involvement.

8. Senge, *The Fifth Discipline*, 218.

9. Stevens, "A Half-Liberated Laity," 2.

10. Powell, *The Nuts and Bolts of Church Growth*, 32.

11. Trueblood, "Learning from Lyle Schaller: Social Aspects of Congregations." *The Christian Century*, January 27, 1993, 82–84.

12. George, *Prepare Your Church for the Future*, 59–60.

13. Barna, *Without a Vision*, 78.

14. Hadaway, *Church Growth Principles*, 157.

15. Callahan, *Twelve Keys to an Effective Church*, 80.

CHAPTER NINE

1. Steiner, *Strategic Planning*, 351.

2. Here are some of the indications of innovativeness that were observed by the three judges in the congregations under study:

• Parents were more likely to respond to requests for assistance.

• More youth leaders were likely to attend district or conference workshops.

• More innovative approaches to worship were in evidence at youth gatherings.

3. Yankelovitch, "How Public Opinion Really Works," 102–108.

4. Spencer, *Winning Through Participation*, 34.

5. Glaser, Abelson, and Garrison, *Putting Knowledge to Work*, 216.

6. Because Worksheet III is limited in what it provides for long-range planning, a task force may wish to secure a planning guide for an entire year. Such a guide, Visionpak, is available from Augsburg Youth and Family Institute (Campus Box 70, Augsburg College, 2211 Riverside Avenue, Minneapolis, MN 55454–1351; 612/330–1624).

Visionpak uses a fifty-two-week calendar, so ideas and action steps can be filled in weekly. This unique booklet allows a committee to look at a vision for one year and see the steps in the planning process. The booklet helps a committee focus not only on the motivating vision but also on their source of guidance and strength. It does this by supplying for each week a scripture verse, a question for reflection, and a suggested prayer.

CHAPTER TEN

1. Schein, *Organizational Culture and Leadership*, 191.

2. Senge, *The Fifth Discipline*, 237.

3. Ibid. 243.

4. Ibid. 246.

5. Glaser, Abelson, and Garrison, *Putting Knowledge to Use*, 61.

6. Hutcheson, *Wheel within the Wheel*, 206.

7. These descriptions of innovative activities show relatively high correlations with the three-item measure In-service Training. The correlations range

from 0.41 to 0.47 to indicate that congregations whose members are involved in training events are more innovative and progressive in their ministries.

8. 4-H groups scoring high on this measure were distinctive in the innovative approaches they made to camping as well as the creative ways they developed for communicating with constituency groups. Apparently, in-service training encourages leaders to be attentive to staying in touch with the people they serve.

In Catholic parochial schools where such training was especially emphasized, we found more of the teachers being stimulated by books, informal sharing opportunities, and seminars. Likewise, their school administrators were more proactive with respect to new programs and staff development activities.

9. The power of in-service training for parochial schools is seen in the fact that the descriptions of innovative activities (listed in the paragraph), correlated at a very high level with the three-item measure, In-service Training. All of the correlations range from 0.70 to 0.75.

10. George, *Prepare Your Church for the Future,* 189.

11. Presbyterian Research Services, *A Study of Elders' Experiences on Session,* 11, tables 9, 10.

12. Olsen, *Transforming Church Boards,* xi, 60–65.

BIBLIOGRAPHY

Adams, John D. *Transforming Leadership: From Vision to Results.* Alexandria, Va.: Miles River Press, 1986.

Allen, Martha Sawyer. "Church Learns from Bible's Teaching on Tithing." *Star Tribune*, November 22, 1996.

Barabba, Vincent P., and Gerald Zaltman. *Hearing the Voice of the Market.* Boston: Harvard Business School Press, 1991.

Barna, George. *Without a Vision, the People Perish.* Glendale, Calif.: Barna Research, 1991.

_____. *Turning Vision into Action.* Ventura, Calif.: Regal Books, 1996.

Beal, George M., Wimal Dissanayake, and Sumiye Koonoshima. *Knowledge Generation, Exchange, and Utilization.* Boulder, Colo.: Westview Press, 1986.

Bennett, William J. "Redeeming the Time,"*Imprimis* 24, no. 11 (November 1995).

Benson, Peter. *Effective Christian Education: A National Study of Protestant Congregations.* Minneapolis: Search Institute, 1990.

Benson, Peter L., Eugene C. Roehlkepartain, and Shelby Andress. *Congregations at Crossroads.* Minneapolis: Search Institute, 1995.

Benson, Peter, and Dorothy Williams. *Religion on Capitol Hill: Myths and Realities.* San Francisco: Harper and Row, 1982.

Bosch, David J. *Transforming Mission.* Maryknoll, New York: Orbis Books, 1992.

Bryson, John M., and Barbara C. Crosby. *Leadership for the Common Good.* San Francisco: Jossey-Bass, 1992.

Buttry, Daniel. *Bringing Your Church Back to Life.* Valley Forge, Pa.: Judson Press, 1988.

Callahan, Kennon L. *Twelve Keys to an Effective Church.* San Francisco: Harper Collins Publisher, 1983.

_____. *Effective Church Leadership: Building on the Twelve Keys.* San Francisco: Harper and Row, 1990.

Carlzon, Jan. *Moments of Truth.* New York: Harper and Row, 1989.

Davis, Howard. "Change and Innovation." In *The Administration of Mental Health Services*, edited by S. Feldman. Springfield, Ill.: Charles C. Thomas, 1973.

Fisher, Roger, and Scott Brown. *Getting Together: Building Relationships as We Negotiate.* New York: Penguin Books, 1989.

George, Carl F. *Prepare Your Church for the Future.* Grand Rapids, Mich.: Fleming H. Revell, 1992.

Glaser, Edward M., Harold H. Abelson, and Kathalee N. Garrison. *Putting Knowledge to Use.* San Francisco: Jossey-Bass Publishers, 1983.

Glover, Robert F., Jose Abraham DeJesus, and Merton P. Strommen. *Congregational Site Visit Reports.* Indianapolis, Ind.: Christian Church (Disciples of Christ), 1990.

Goleman, Daniel. *Emotional Intelligence. Why It Can Matter More than IQ.* New York: Bantam Books, 1995.

Hadaway, C. Kirk. *Church Growth Principles.* Nashville: Broadman Press, 1991.

Hale, Sandra and Mary Williams, eds. *Managing Change: A Guide to Producing Innovation from Within.* Washington, D.C.: Urban Institute Press, 1989.

Hogan, Robert. "Trouble at the Top: Causes and Consequences of Managerial Incompetence." *Journal of Consulting Psychology* 46, no. 1 (Winter 1994): 9–15.

Hulstrand, Eric. "Pioneering on the Prairie." *The Lutheran,* August 1996, 6–7.

Hunter, George G. *How to Reach Secular People.* Nashville: Abingdon Press, 1992.

Hutcheson, Richard G. *Wheel within the Wheel.* Atlanta: John Knox Press, 1979.

Imai, Masaaki. *KAIZEN.* New York: McGraw-Hill Publishing, 1986.

Inskeep, Kenneth W., and Kathryn Sime. *Effective Ministry and Membership Growth.* Chicago: Evangelical Lutheran Church in America, 1996.

Johnston, Douglas, and Cynthia Sampson, eds. *Religion: The Missing Dimension of Statecraft.* New York: Oxford University Press, 1994.

Klaas, Alan C., and Cheryl D. Brown. *Church Membership Initiative.* Appleton, Wis.: Aid Association for Lutherans, 1994.

Kouzes, James M., and Barry Z. Posner. *The Leadership Challenge.* San Francisco: Jossey-Bass, 1991.

Krueger, Richard A. *Focus Groups.* Newbury, Calif.: Sage Publications, 1988.

Kuenning, Paul P. *Rise and Fall of American Lutheran Pietism.* Macon, Ga.: Mercer University Press, 1988.

Kurpius, DeWayne J., Dale R. Fuqua, and Thaddeus G. Rozecki. "The Power of Consultants Conceptual Thinking: Paradigms, Models, and Processes." *Journal of Consulting Psychology* 43, no. 3 (Fall 1991): 2–10.

Lippitt, Ronald. "Future Before You Plan." *The NTL Manager's Handbook.*

———. "Utilizing Resistance as a Resource for Change." Unpublished paper.

Luecke, David S. *The Other Story of Lutherans at Worship.* Tempe, Ariz.: Fellowship Ministries, 1995.

Machiavelli, Nicolo. *The Prince.* Translated by George Bull. Baltimore: Penguin Books, 1961.

Mead, Loren B. *The Once and Future Church: Reinventing the Congregation for a New Mission Frontier.* Washington, D.C.: The Alban Institute, 1991.

———. *More Than Numbers: The Ways Churches Grow.* Washington D.C.: The Alban Institute, 1993.

Monroe, Kelly. *Finding God at Harvard.* Grand Rapids, Mich.: Zondervan Publishing House, 1996.

Nicholi, Armand, Jr. "Hope in a Secular Age." *In Finding God at Harvard.* Edited by Kelly Monroe. Grand Rapids, Mich.: Zondervan, 1996.

Niebuhr, Gustav. "In Isolated U.S. Churches, Innovative Plans Fill Pulpits." *New York Times,* March 12, 1995.

Olsen, Charles M. *Transforming Church Boards into Communities of Spiritual Leaders.* Bethesda, Md.: The Alban Institute, 1995.

Olson, Daniel V. A. "Learning from Lyle Schaller: Social Aspects of Congregations." *The Christian Century*, January 27, 1993, 82–84.

Peters, Thomas J., and Robert Waterman. *In Search of Excellence*. New York: Harper & Row, 1982.

Presbyterian Research Services. *A Study of Elders' Experiences on Session*. Louisville, Ky.: Presbyterian Church (U.S.A.), 1994.

Rogers, Everett M. *Diffusion of Innovations*. 3rd ed. New York: The Free Press, 1983.

_____. *Communication Technology*. New York: The Free Press, 1986.

Ronsvalle, John, and Sylvia Ronsvalle. "The End of Benevolence? Alarming Trends in Church Giving." *The Christian Century*, October 23, 1996, 1010–1014.

Ross, Richard. *Planning Youth Ministry from Boot-up to Exit*. Nashville: Broadman Press, 1997.

Schein, Edgar H. *Organizational Culture and Leadership*. San Francisco: Jossey-Bass, 1991.

Schneider, William. E. "Productivity Improvement through Cultural Focus." *Journal of Consulting Psychology* 47, no. 1 (Winter 1995): 3–27.

Schuller, David S., Merton P. Strommen, and Milo L. Brekke. *Ministry in America*. San Francisco: Harper and Row, 1980.

Schuller, Robert H. *Your Church Has a Fantastic Future*. Ventura: Regal Books, 1986.

Search Institute. *Your Congregation's Future* (video). Minneapolis: Search Institute, 1996.

Senge, Peter M. *The Fifth Discipline*. New York: Doubleday, 1990.

Senge, Peter M., et al. *The Fifth Discipline Fieldbook*. New York: Doubleday, 1994.

Shawchuck, Norman, Philip Kotler, Bruce Wrenn, and Gustave Rath. *Marketing for Congregations*. Nashville: Abingdon Press, 1992.

Spencer, Laura J. *Winning Through Participation*. Dubuque, Iowa: Kendall-Hunt Publishing, 1989.

Steiner, George A. *Strategic Planning*. New York: The Free Press, 1979.

Stevens, Paul R. "A Half-Liberated Laity." *Laity Exchange*, September 1989, 1–6.

Strommen, Merton P. *Five Cries of Youth*. San Francisco: Harper Collins, 1991.

_____. *Research on Religious Development: A Comprehensive Handbook*. New York: Hawthorn Books Inc., 1971.

Strommen, Merton P., Milo Brekke, Ralph Underwager, and Arthur Johnson. *A Study of Generations*. Minneapolis: Augsburg Publishing House, 1972.

Strommen, Merton P., and Shelby Andress. *Five Shaping Forces*. Washington, D.C.: National Catholic Educational Association, 1980.

Strommen, Merton P., and Irene H. Strommen. *Five Cries of Parents*. Minneapolis: Augsburg Youth and Family Institute, 1993.

Strommen, Peter E. *Vision Statement for First Lutheran Church*, Duluth, Minnesota. Unpublished paper, 1993.

Towns, Elmer L. *Ten of Today's Most Innovative Churches*. Ventura, Calif.: Regal Books, 1990.

Warren, Rick. *The Purpose Driven Church*. Grand Rapids, Mich.: Zondervan Publishing House, 1995.

Waterman, Robert H. *Adhocracy.* New York: W. W. Norton Co., 1992.

Wink, Walter. *Unmasking the Powers: The Invisible Forces that Determine Human Existence.* Philadelphia: Fortress Press, 1986.

Yankelovitch, Daniel. "How Public Opinion Really Works." *Fortune,* October 5, 1992, 102–108.

Zaltman, Gerald, and R. Duncan. *Strategies for Planned Change.* New York: John Wiley and Sons, 1977.

Zaltman, Gerald, D. Florio, and L. Sikorski. *Dynamic Educational Change: Models, Strategies, Tactics, and Management.* New York: John Wiley and Sons, 1977.